Non-Profit/
Pro-Growth

# THE **KVC** STORY

Improving Child Welfare Through
Values-Based Organizational Growth

# PRAISE FOR
## *Non-Profit/Pro-Growth —*
## *The KVC Story*

"A wise and invaluable book about what it takes to lead in the most difficult and important of settings. Mr. Sims has written a book about leadership within non-profit organizations in the child welfare system, based on his experience over many years as CEO of KVC, one of the largest non-profit child welfare organizations in the nation. The book is infused with a tremendous depth of experience from an author with a track record of considerable accomplishment in the non-profit sector. The ideas presented are so compelling because they are forged from hard lessons in the real world. And the ideas inspire. They demonstrate that effective leadership requires more than just strategy and business sense: it requires heart, and soul, and values, and basic human decency. This book provides terrific principles for leadership that should be understood by all those who aspire to leadership, irrespective of the sector of the organization they aspire to lead."

**Glenn Saxe, MD**
Professor, Department of Child and Adolescent Psychiatry
New York University School of Medicine

"Much more than a memoir of the remarkable career of a truly visionary leader, *Non-Profit/Pro-Growth — The KVC Story* is a compelling, highly readable, and practical guide for anyone working to change how human services are delivered. Rich in examples, this book captures hard-earned lessons in strategic planning, management, leadership development, and the often-neglected challenges of implementation. Everyone working to improve care for children, from frontline staff to supervisors to agency directors to policy makers, should read and then re-read this book."

**Patrick McCarthy, PhD**
President of the Annie E. Casey Foundation (Baltimore, MD)


"Long before the term 'social entrepreneur' came into popular usage, Wayne Sims was defining what it means. This book is a tremendous resource for readers interested in what it really takes to build a great company from the ground up in the nonprofit sector. Mr. Sims takes us inside the development of the KVC magic, and shares the hard business decisions and financial risks taken to build a nationwide organization that is driven by higher-purpose values and grounded in science-based practice. The book is also a testament to the gritty perseverance and vision that leadership demands. By staying true to responding to the actual needs of maltreated children and families, Mr. Sims stayed faithful to his ideals and built a legacy that will benefit America for decades to come.

I highly recommend that social work and other human service educators use this book with their students to help prepare them for the tough but exciting realities of contemporary leadership."

**Jim Clark, PhD, LCSW**
Dean & Professor, Florida State University College of Social Work

"Wayne's book is a must-read by any emerging leader in our field and sector. The story of KVC and the highly relevant and transferrable 'lessons learned' shared by Wayne demonstrate how our sector is more than providers of great programs and services under contract with government. We are transformational agents of change. KVC shows all of us that it is through steadfastness in our belief that all people should have the opportunity to live their lives to their fullest potential that our sector shines bright in American today. Wayne's account of KVC's history and focus on the future demonstrates this beautifully. Leaders and organizations achieving breakthrough results and success are the ones who are steadfast in their values; are disruptive to status quo; are humble about what they do not know; are inquisitive and innovative, courageous, and generous in spirit; and are always focused through their advocacy on making systems work better for all children, adults and families."

**Susan N. Dreyfus**
President and CEO of the Alliance for Strong Families and Communities, and Former Secretary of the Washington State Department of Social and Health Services


"A true testament to the impact people can achieve when driven by a vision of making the world a better place. Wayne Sims reminds us the KVC story is about people, unwavering values and the commitment to help vulnerable families build hope and resiliency. We owe Wayne a tremendous amount of gratitude for his vision and dedication to communities, and for sharing with us the measure of a true leader."

**Jason Hooper**
CEO, KVC Health Systems

# THE **KVC** STORY

Non-Profit/
Pro-Growth

Improving Child Welfare Through
Values-Based Organizational Growth

B. Wayne Sims

Editing by:
Anne Roberts
Joyce White
Cathy Dorton Fyock
Mark Ray
Kate Colbert

Cover design and typesetting by:
Courtney Hudson

First edition, October 2017

ISBN: 978-0-9991491-0-2

Library of Congress Control Number: 2017951709

Created in the United States of America

# TABLE OF CONTENTS

# 1

# More Than 40 Years of Learning

More than 40 years ago, I began a magnificent journey in the remarkable fields of behavioral healthcare and child welfare. Along the way, I had the opportunity to obtain an amazing experiential education that truly augmented my academic background in clinical psychology and healthcare administration. The initial path set at KVC was predicated on my earlier work experience and will be highlighted in this book. These early work experiences permeated my intense drive as KVC began to evolve. As time passed, a course was charted, and with the help of many, the organization was propelled into national and international prominence.

I started at Wyandotte House, Inc., in 1980 with five vulnerable youths in care whose parents had all had their parental rights severed by the court system. These youths marked the transition into what is now KVC Health Systems. As the organization began to grow outside of Wyandotte County, Kansas, we felt it was necessary to change the name to be more reflective of a larger, more comprehensive organization. Initially, the name was changed to Kaw Valley Center, but we subsequently outgrew that region as well. Ultimately, we changed the name to KVC Health Systems with the KVC, which was now an important part of our identity, representing our commitment to Knowledge, Values, and Connections.

KVC has grown from a small, struggling non-profit children's organization into a nationally and internationally known leader in the fields of child welfare and behavioral healthcare. It has grown from a staff of five to nearly 1,400, from providing services in one county to serving multiple states and offering training in other countries, and from an annual budget of about $220,000 to nearly $150 million. Our mission and vision have spread and dramatically broadened our service delivery system. KVC makes the promise that we, as an organization, will enrich and enhance the lives of children, adults, and their families through medical, education, social welfare, and behavioral health services.

In this book, I hope to share some of my lessons learned and to acknowledge those who helped KVC Health Systems become the dynamic organization it is today. I will cite some strategic planning and share stories that, when woven together, became the fabric of KVC, setting it apart from a host of other good organizations. While this book is as accurate as I can make it, some of the information represents my memories and opinions. Although my story is about one organization, I hope the many examples used will be helpful to other entities, whether non-profit or for-profit.

I was mesmerized the first time I read this quote by George Bernard Shaw: "Some men see things as they are and say, 'Why?' Others dream things that never were and say, 'Why not?'" This is a quote I have thought about during much of my adult life, and it has certainly helped to motivate me as I have hoped to motivate others around me. Throughout this book, I have included many quotations that I have personally found to be motivating, and I have passed these on to others. In the same manner, I have tried to create brief statements that, when replicated, might help teach values. From those value statements and others, a culture was developed at KVC that did not focus on what was but, rather, on what might be. Over the years, others have added to these sayings, which we began calling our "isms." These represent our values.

## "Whatever limits us we call fate."

— Ralph Waldo Emerson —

The early journey at KVC will be referenced to bring clarity to decisions made and challenges overcome. Ralph Waldo Emerson said, "Whatever limits us we call fate." Through this journey, many of the limitations we faced were complex, but by staying the course, we overcame most. Form, it's said, follows function. In our case, the foundation for KVC was based on value statements we not only believed but followed as we changed the way foster care and behavioral healthcare were delivered to vulnerable children and families. By not accepting the limits we faced as our fate, we created our own future.

# 2

# Gratitude

"Dance with the ones who brought you." Using this advice, I would have danced all night with so many. And if you have actually danced with me, you understand it would have been a long night. Throughout my career, I have been fortunate to have crossed paths with many talented and supportive individuals. Some were professionals in my fields. Others, from different careers, seemed almost divinely placed in my path. In either scenario, I both learned from and modeled their actions and deeds. Let me begin expressing my gratitude for my parents, very good people who started me off well with a sense of purpose and a value system that included a knowledge of right and wrong and a concern for others.

Of course, I want to thank my wife and two daughters for their love and compassion blended with just the right amount of patience. I often think of KVC as my third child, and I appreciate the willingness of my daughters to share me with this additional child.

In like fashion, I thank the very supportive and talented board members who have served, at one time or another, throughout this past generation. I would also like to recognize the army of avid and highly motivated volunteers and business partners who have given of their time, talent, and treasure. Without this level of support, KVC would never have become the organization that it is today.

It is impossible not to mention the role of the Junior League and its membership, as they were responsible for starting our predecessor organization, Wyandotte House. The enormity of what Ellen McCarthy did to identify the original need and her continued lifetime of dedication could only be paralleled by the support provided by JoAnn Ball following its founding. JoAnn, in her role on the KVC Board of Directors, brought her entire family to the organization in meaningful ways. Her family members have subsequently contributed to the success of KVC and remain strongly involved today, and I owe them all immense gratitude.

I can truly say that KVC has been blessed with quality board members. Many offered not only wisdom and support but, in their own ways, worked to make life better for children in need. Both Dick Bond and Fred Ball were KVC board members who were immensely special to me. They freely gave of their time, and each provided me with a quality "sounding board." When growing an organization or business, there are always roadblocks and obstacles with which to contend. Rarely does someone in my position have the luxury of such talented advice givers, mentors, and friends.

---

**"The best executive is the one who has sense enough to pick good people to do what he wants done, and self-restraint enough to keep from meddling with them while they do it."**

— Theodore Roosevelt —

---

I am extremely proud of the quality, commitment, and passion of the KVC staff. At the top was a group of C-suite executives and management team members that any non-profit or for-profit company would envy. I was truly blessed to have worked with my immediate executive team members who represented an average of 28 years with KVC by the time of my retirement. Rarely, if ever, do CEOs get a chance to work with such talented people and for as long as I did. I credit much of our success to their leadership. I have often said that good CEOs surround themselves with individuals at least as intelligent as themselves and, if they're smart, individuals who are even more intelligent. Theodore Roosevelt said, "The best executive is the one who has sense enough to pick good people to do what he wants done, and self-restraint enough to keep from meddling with them while they do it." I always felt that I had been drawn to KVC for some greater purpose. It may have been only a belief system that my parents had inculcated in me as a child; nonetheless, together with a great team we were able to achieve goals and outcomes that many said were impossible.

---

**"Character cannot be developed in ease and quiet. Only through experience of trial and suffering can the soul be strengthened, ambition inspired, and success achieved."**

— Helen Keller —

---

According to Helen Keller, "Character cannot be developed in ease and quiet. Only through experience of trial and suffering can the soul be strengthened, ambition inspired, and success achieved." My "C's" helped me to define our organization's character: Anne Roberts, chief operations officer; Paul Klayder, chief financial officer; and Sherry Love, chief clinical officer. Together we drove successful initiatives, endured painful experiences, and in doing so built an organization of which we are proud.

Each of these executives was handpicked not only for his or her skillset but for his or her personal character. Each had an internal drive that was endowed with deep-seated values. For example, Paul Klayder managed KVC's finances as if they were his own. With his impeccable honesty, advanced skills, and unwavering commitment to holding a hard line on expenses, Paul kept KVC viable throughout its history. I think he must have felt, many times, as if he were on a listing ship where only he could create the necessary equilibrium. All KVC leadership did what they could do to get Paul's praise; it was a special commodity rarely displayed but always cherished.

---

♥ KVC-ism

### *Every interaction is an intervention!*

---

Sherry Love served as our chief clinical officer and was extremely intense about everything she did. She was a perfectionist and was tenacious about making sure we were deploying the latest research. As purveyors and researchers were often on the coasts and weren't always interested in the Midwest, Sherry would literally stalk them at conferences until she could get their attention, with the intent of learning strategies she felt would be beneficial to our children and families. While others with varying degrees of talent may have settled for less, thinking they were already working extremely hard, Sherry never wavered in her quest. Sherry added *Every Interaction Is an Intervention* to the KVC-isms!

In addition, our success was predicated on another variable: Anne Roberts. I really cannot say enough about her. Without Anne, I doubt seriously whether we could have accomplished what we did. She worked tirelessly on every service we delivered. From the beginning, I saw superb talent in her. During her initial job interview, more than 30 years earlier, she competed against more experienced candidates and at least one with a PhD. However, Anne had an authentic personality with unwavering values, which could be seen even then. She believed, as did I, that we must treat every child and family as we'd want our own treated and that excellence is not an act, but a habit. From the very beginning, she shared my vision of a better system for children and families and of the importance of continual growth. Anne helped shape it, added to it, and demanded only the best from our staff. I am thoroughly indebted to her.

In addition to a great group of "C's" was my executive assistant, Joyce White, who was capable of almost reading my mind. She is extremely talented and was on call seven days a week, 365 days a year. In a time when many people see their jobs as only a means for earning a living, Joyce understood me as well as the mission and was always ready to assist. She was a rare asset that I valued greatly.

I also want to acknowledge my management team, a superior group of subsidiary presidents, executive vice presidents, and other key leaders who represent the ongoing development of tremendous bench depth within the organization. They, along with all of our dedicated staff, are the future of KVC. Specifically, one member of the management team, Jason Hooper, embraced the vision early. Starting with KVC after college graduation, Jason had the opportunity to experience several different positions, but what stood out early was his conviction to our mission. As I did with other young and talented leaders, I gave him an assortment of jobs with graduated levels of difficulty; he triumphed in each of these roles. He continually demonstrated knowledge of our vision and mission, and he displayed our values to peers and other staff every day. I'm sure it was a shock to no one that Jason became the subsequent CEO.

Writing this book has been a very cathartic experience for me. There have been so many individuals who touched and helped shape the organization we now know, and it is impossible to name them all. If I'd attempted to do so, I fear the book would have been twice as long. Thank you all for the vital roles you played.

# 3

# My Life Before KVC

My earliest experiential learning came from two social workers — Fred Tully and David Loving, who held leadership positions at a state institution in Iowa — and a noted psychiatrist, Richard Jenkins, MD. Fred and David were both very dynamic individuals who could easily influence others. They were enormously talented and accomplished much. From them, I learned to try to keep a happy heart and an awareness of presentation even in the midst of the many painful trials and experiences that accompany this field. And I still try to emulate their adamant approach to doing what is right.

Perhaps my greatest — and most painful — early learning came from Dr. Jenkins. It occurred during my first patient review in the 1970s, when I was fresh out of graduate school and working as a psychologist at a state institution in Iowa. The person chairing that staffing was Dr. Jenkins. As I learned later, he was a nationally known psychiatrist and researcher who had spent much of his life studying child behavior and who was a major contributor to the *Diagnostic and Statistical Manual* (DSM). He had graduated from Stanford University and obtained his MD from the University of Chicago. After holding several noted research positions, he had become chair of the Child Psychiatry Department at the University of Iowa. Later in his life, he stepped down from his role as department chair, accepted an emeritus position at the university, and started work at the institution where my career began.

At that state institution in Iowa, I had been assigned a caseload of patients and was informed that I was to present at a staffing on a mid-teen adolescent. As I started to present my case, Dr. Jenkins immediately began asking me a series of questions. Unfortunately, I could not answer all of his questions without referencing this young man's file. After a short interval, Dr. Jenkins stopped the staffing and asked me to leave. He told me not to come back until I knew everything there was to know about this patient. Then he proceeded to go on with other cases to be presented that day. Needless to say, I was sufficiently embarrassed.

---

## "There is nothing good or bad but thinking makes it so."

— William Shakespeare —

---

So how do you process that learning? I could have immediately started looking for a new job. I could have complained that I was new and did not understand what was expected. (I had staffed cases at the university before, and no one had ever stopped me or complained that I was doing anything wrong.) I could also have reacted angrily, gotten upset, and let it be known that I should not have been treated that way. Shakespeare said, "There is nothing good or bad but thinking makes it so."

What I did, however, was to acknowledge that I was a new employee fresh out of graduate school who did not know everything. I chose to try to learn from others who had much more experience, and I began to appreciate what Dr. Jenkins was saying. If I was going to be helpful to the individuals I was treating, then I needed to know everything relevant to their lives. Dr. Jenkins was very focused on knowing the entire family constellation, including the extended family history. This was a long time before I ever heard of a genogram.

Dr. Jenkins never had to ask me to leave again, as I never went into another staffing without knowing everything there was to know about my patients. I later often referenced this to employees as an example of "one-time learning." You can have 10 years of experience or one year of experience 10 times.

Later, Dr. Jenkins and I actually became close colleagues. A handful of other young 20-something professionals and I would occasionally meet with him in the evening at one of our homes to discuss different theorists and their corresponding research and the latest treatment methodologies. At the time, Dr. Jenkins was in his early 70s and had personally known all of the major theorists whom we had studied in graduate school. It was an amazing experience that I would have missed had I not been able to get past my initial indignation.

So, what is the lesson here? I have found over time that much of our quality learning comes from hard teachers and bad experiences. Generally speaking, the good experiences do not linger like bad ones. Thus, most of our learning, I suspect, comes from negative experiences. Again, what appears negative at the time may actually be beneficial to you over time. This is a hard lesson to learn but one that I have experienced many times. If we learn to check our egos at the door, we can greatly enrich our professional education.

Entry-level positions provide excellent learning opportunities. I believe it was my eagerness to learn at each level that resulted in my promotions into upper-level management within five years after starting employment at that state institution. I think my experience shows what those in decision-making positions are looking for in young employees. Do they approach their jobs enthusiastically and try to learn all they can about each position? Employees who embrace learning and growing within each position they hold, most often, get promoted.

While I was still in my first professional job at the state institution in Iowa and had just been promoted to be in charge of all program services, I became focused on how we received our new admissions. What I found was that a court official or a district attorney would call to indicate that a new admission would be coming. We never had the opportunity to pick and choose which admissions we were interested in accepting. It made no difference if we had significant assessment or background information or if none was available. This was a great lesson to learn. We had to be ready to admit all referrals immediately, no matter what physical size they were, what egregious behaviors they had shown, or what diagnoses they had been given. In fact, during my tenure there, at least five adolescents were court-ordered to the institution for committing a homicide. There would just be a call, and a new emotionally troubled youth would appear that day. Or maybe there would be five calls, and then five new youths would appear.

I eventually learned that this was a foreign concept in the child welfare field. There, most group homes and residential facilities, whether or not they provide treatment services, have the opportunity to accept or reject any and every referral. Unfortunately, adolescents who were often turned down from several facilities would be referred to an out-of-state facility. Later in my career, I would find that this was true in many or most states, as I will speak to throughout this book.

But my learning began at that state institution. And it was quality learning, including the admission practice of "no reject, no eject," of serving each child referred who needed our care as opposed to screening out or discharging those with challenges deemed too severe. I later used this philosophy to impact child welfare practices in Kansas and other states where we worked. As of this writing (in 2017), sending children out of state for services is still a practice in some states, although not in

Kansas. No state custodial children or youths are referred out of state for treatment purposes — at least none in the 50 percent of the state KVC has been contracted to manage.

I experienced one extreme but painful example of learning while in my administrative role at the state institution: A 13-year-old adolescent boy successfully hanged himself in his room. While the medical staff and other staff on duty did what they could do to save this young man, he eventually succumbed. A nurse who was making rounds that day had stopped to talk with a behavioral health technician for only a couple of minutes. In that time, this child had wrapped a piece of clothing around a doorknob and his neck and dropped to his knees.

Those who had worked closely with him felt that he was not truly suicidal but was merely "gesturing." Many felt he knew exactly when the nurse would be making rounds and likely thought that she would catch him in time. This so-called gesturing, sadly, went too far because when he dropped to his knees, he apparently could not get back on his feet. Gesturing then became a term I disliked immensely, even though it was used commonly in the profession. To me, anyone who gestured was someone capable of committing suicide. When something like this occurs, you are changed forever. Unfortunately, many of us in the field, as well as those in the accrediting bodies, learned the hard way that doorknobs were inappropriate and certainly not safe in a psychiatric setting. Each facility I have overseen since, and every administrator I subsequently appointed over such a facility, has been charged with ensuring the latest safety features and the most stringent super-vision possible.

A couple of years later, I left the state institution to become the execu-tive director of a relatively large community mental health center, also located in Iowa. Again, this role produced great learning for me. As with any leadership position, there were many applicants. After the selection process had been concluded and I had been hired, I asked why I was chosen over the other applicants. I was told that the prior executive director and the prior medical director had both been fired. Each had a faction of the staff supporting him, and little was being accomplished due to frequent disagreements among the staff. Board members were also siding with one director or the other. One of the questions asked of each candidate was, "What would you do to prevent this from reoccurring?" Apparently, other applicants went into great detail about how they would have frequent staff meetings to attempt mediation. I was told that a primary reason I was selected was that I was the only one who said not to make the executive director and medical director roles parallel positions. I had suggested creating a chain of command by putting the medical director under the executive director, which would alleviate the problem. From then on, the medical director worked under the executive director. This represented an early example in my career where I needed to be decisive, even when controversial, and think beyond the status quo when change was needed.

That was also my first experience working with a board of directors. It was the only time I was interviewed by the entire board in one afternoon and by the entire staff the following morning. It was a grueling experience but one that was very formative in my leadership and in my on-the-job training process at a young age. The 25-member board was composed of civic leaders, patients of the center, and others with an interest in mental health. The members of this board had taken sides with either the medical director or the executive director. This was the first time in my life that I became very familiar with the prayer of serenity. I had to learn which things to accept, which things I could change, and, of course, how to know the difference.

The community mental health center was like the state institution in one respect: Every referral was accepted and was assigned a therapist. No one was turned away. As was true with most outpatient settings, most of the staff preferred seeing patients in their offices. For patients ready to transition from the state hospital to their homes, few staff members were interested in visiting them in the hospital or their homes and in supporting their return to the community. So I assumed that responsibility. This experience further reinforced the importance of meeting with patients in their own homes or communities, where change must occur, and not in isolation.

As I mentioned before, some learning can be good, some can be bad, and some can be humorous. Perhaps the funniest experience I had at the community mental health center was being called by a police officer to come to the police station to get one of our psychiatrists released from custody. Apparently, he had been caught stealing an expensive sport coat. He explained the incident and paid for the coat, and all was forgiven by authorities — but not by me. This incident reinforced for me the importance of hiring for character and not just degrees.

Perhaps my worst experience in this position was being on call one weekend and having a patient I was not familiar with call to say she was going to commit suicide. I talked with her and encouraged her to go to the hospital emergency room, where I would meet her. She refused and said she was going to commit suicide, then hung up on me. This was in the days before cell phones and electronic medical records, so I raced to the mental health center, where I pulled her file, retrieved her address and phone number, and attempted to call her back. Not being able to reach her immediately, I then called the police chief, whom I knew, and asked him to have an officer join me at this lady's apartment. I also called her regular therapist for more information. He was more than a little upset that I was calling him to learn more about his patient. He had been watching a movie and was missing "a good part" and indicated that she was probably just "gesturing."

The officer and I arrived at the apartment at about the same time and were seconds from getting the apartment building manager to open the door. As that was happening, and as luck would have it, the woman I had spoken with came around a hallway corner and asked what we were doing. As I began speaking to her, she recognized my voice and began crying. Afterward, she went with me to the hospital and began talking to me about all of the very bad things that had happened to her and why she was so clinically depressed. The following Monday morning, I had a long counseling session with her assigned therapist.

Another very educational experience at the community mental health center occurred one morning as I was sitting in my office. Three Secret Service officers appeared at my assistant's office wanting to speak to me. They had appropriate documentation and were interested in the clinical records of a chronically mentally ill patient who had an extensive mental health history and who had been at the state hospital on multiple occasions for stabilization. This was in 1979, and the 1980 election season had already opened. Jimmy Carter was president, and Ted Kennedy was the leading challenger for the Democratic Party's nomination. Iowa has always been in the forefront of presidential elections, and Kennedy was scheduled to speak in the city later that week.

Only about a decade earlier, our country had gone through the turmoil brought on by those trying to influence history by assassinating leaders who did not represent their interests. Both Martin Luther King, Jr., and Bobby Kennedy had been felled by a gunman's bullet. I was young but remembered an announcement over the school's intercom system saying that John Kennedy had been shot. And then I was awakened in 1968 by my clock radio bellowing out that Bobby Kennedy had been shot in California.

Now the remaining Kennedy brother was coming to my city, and a patient from my center had written letters stating that he intended to kill him. When the agents visited, I immediately had a sickening feeling. I was determined not to be a bit player in another Kennedy brother's tragedy. The gentleman who wrote these threatening letters was not a person whom I believed would actually go through with his threat to kill Mr. Kennedy, but I had learned earlier that gesturing of any kind may result in an action that could produce a horrific outcome. I cooperated fully, and the gentleman was questioned and briefly detained.

Whether another tragedy was actually avoided by those efforts, I will never know. I did know that Ted Kennedy was receiving threats from other mentally unstable individuals from across the country. I would never sit idly by when I thought there might be something I could do to prevent even the smallest of potentially harmful acts. My mother had mentioned more than once to me as a child that an ounce of prevention is worth more than a pound of cure. That lesson has served me well by prompting me to always look ahead for potential problems and then try to prevent them from ever occurring. In the fields of child welfare and behavioral healthcare, we meet at the juncture of hurt and heartache each time a child is removed from his or her family into foster care or each time a member of a family is hospitalized. The unique situations in these fields often present many painful challenges for which we must constantly be vigilant.

Again, I reiterate that there is no bad learning. I have always been very cognizant that new learning and new experience are required to keep people fresh in their jobs. I truly believe that, when it comes to careers and to organizations, if you are not growing, you're dying. As cited earlier, I have frequently said that one individual can have 10 years of experience or one year of experience 10 times. Unfortunately, in the latter case, some people experience the same results over and over again but continue to maintain a status quo. They don't actually learn or grow from them. I have always believed in continual learning and growing with each lesson learned. All of the leaders at KVC exemplify that belief.

# 4

## Wyandotte House: The Women

No matter what type of business, there is usually at least one, and often many, good stories behind successful enterprises. KVC is no different. I will try to touch on some of these stories in the chapters to come. However, an obvious one is how the organization got started.

Mahatma Gandhi said, "You must be the change you want to see in the world." Before I was ever introduced to KVC, there was a group of women who saw a need and founded the organization as it was originally known: Wyandotte House, Inc.

---

### "You must be the change you want to see in the world."

— Mahatma Gandhi —

---

Ellen McCarthy, then president of what is now the Junior League of Wyandotte and Johnson Counties, was volunteering at Kaw View Detention Center in 1969. In her art classes, she met children and adolescents being held for actions such as running away from home or for other non-felonious reasons. This prompted Ellen to begin thinking of what could be done to prevent these children from being inappropriately incarcerated. Without her profound sense of what was right and what was wrong, KVC might not have been born.

Ellen and several other women of the League joined forces and began studying options to address this concern. Seeking professional advice, Ellen met with Terry Showalter, then head of the Wyandotte County Juvenile Court Services. Terry advised that they could, in fact, create a group home where youths with needs such as these could be served instead of in the highly structured and punitive confinement in the detention center.

Ellen's and her colleagues' intent was to create a home-like setting for boys who did not have a home or could not stay safely at home. They wanted it to be as typical a setting as possible, so they looked for a home in a neighborhood. This handful of ladies went to a bank and signed for the purchase of the first home. It was called Wyandotte House and was later incorporated as Wyandotte House, Inc. As the story goes, they signed a mortgage for the purchase of this home without mentioning it to their husbands (at least not until years later when it was paid off). Their intention was to hire a husband-and-wife team to serve as the group home parents. Initially, the wife stayed at home, and the husband went to work. The ladies from the League met with the couple on a regular basis to set a budget and to monitor finances. While this was not an easy task, the organization began to find a niche, and soon there was need for another group home. So another was sought out and, again, another mortgage taken. This home, Kiely House, was for girls; its name memorialized a young female juvenile court judge who died too young.

A third home, Logan House, eventually followed. The story behind this house involves a man in the community, Mr. Logan, who lived basically as a hermit with few visible possessions. As the story goes, this man approached a local banker one day with a strange request. Mr. Logan indicated that he was dying and had some money kept in his very small and unpretentious home. Without relatives, Mr. Logan approached the banker and indicated his interest in giving him the money he had saved. The banker suggested to Mr. Logan that he give his money to Wyandotte House, a local charity that he had heard about.

So, the banker, whose name is lost in history, passed along Mr. Logan's hidden savings — which totaled some $45,000 — to Wyandotte House. The ladies were extremely happy to accept this generous donation but worried the state might stop giving them the ongoing financial support they had been receiving for each child placed when it heard about the gift. Of course, the state did not withhold its payments, and Logan House was born.

Each of these homes needed repairs. The story, as told to me, was that the ladies from the Junior League enlisted the young men of a service group called the Jaycees. As a volunteer project, the Jaycees joined forces and readied each home for its young occupants. Without this support, the organization might never have passed the necessary inspections to become a non-profit group-home organization. One of the Jaycees at the time was Gary Grable, a banker who ultimately served a long tenure on the KVC board.

One Junior League member at the time of KVC's birth, JoAnn Ball, knew of the new venture and followed its progress. From the beginning, JoAnn understood and supported the KVC initiatives. Not only did she embrace the vision, she helped drive it by co-chairing our first capital campaign. At a time when the river running through the heart of Kansas City truly separated two states, organizations that were located in Kansas did not fare well with the large philanthropic foundations located in Kansas City, Missouri; none of these organizations wanted to give financial support to Wyandotte County. So, while we were not able to receive philanthropic funds from the foundations, JoAnn helped to introduce our organization to many new donors with financial means. She was of tremendous assistance and was the model for others willing to give of their time, talents, and treasure. There were many other women, such as Betty Crooker, Sue Bond, Joanie Spencer Cooke, Marianne Aiken, Connie Mullinix, and other tireless board members and volunteers who were very instrumental in assisting this young organization.

# 5

# Wyandotte House: The Men

When I came to Wyandotte House in 1980 to accept the CEO position, I found the organization to be in a serious downturn. There was one functioning group home with a handful of clients, another group home open but not accepting referrals, and a third home that had been closed due to damage inflicted by prior clients. At that juncture in our history, the state's social services had stopped making referrals to our organization. It truly was a very bleak time. I knew my immediate role had to involve improving services to clients referred to our organization. I also had to regain the trust of the state's social services. These were not mutually exclusive concepts but improving services had to come first.

I learned almost immediately that I needed to look for someone I could not only trust but who could provide legal counsel as well. Initially, I found the organization to be rather chaotic and not performing up to the level that our board wanted. I found that counsel in Scott Asner, who never gave me anything but good advice. Scott, who is very intelligent, was always available to me and quick to get to the point. Of course, in the early days he knew I was unable to be a paying client, but he remained gracious and accessible to me. I truly thank Scott for his longtime friendship and for his decades of continual support to KVC.

In the late 1990s, my wife and I joined Scott and his wife, Susan, at a Kansas City Royals baseball game, where we were able to enjoy the game while sitting in their superb seats. During the game, Susan and I started to double-team Scott about becoming more active again with KVC. With Scott having a business interest in the beautiful and challenging National Golf Course, we began discussing a golf tournament as a fundraising event. That evening, the annual KVC Kids Golf Classic was born. In the years since, there has been a steady, dramatic increase in participation and in revenues, rising well into six figures annually. For the past several years, the tournament has not only been a sell-out but has expanded from only morning sessions to both morning and afternoon sessions. I owe tremendous thanks to Scott and Susan for their combined decades of hard work and dedication in support of KVC's mission and vision.

---

## "Only a life lived for others is a life worth living."

— Albert Einstein —

---

There were two other individuals who not only offered wisdom but whose cups overflowed with commonsense and an abundance of friendship. When I think of them, I also think about a quote from Albert Einstein, who said, "Only a life lived for others is a life worth living." I can't think of a better descriptor than that for these two earthly giants: Fred Ball and Dick Bond. Both of these gentlemen had tremendous careers and were hugely successful in their respective lives. I would use the words kindness, compassion, competence, and generosity as personal characteristics of these men.

I've always liked the story of the young man who was walking on the beach, picking up starfish, and throwing them back into the ocean. While the young man was doing this, he was approached by a passerby who reminded him that there were miles and miles of beach and that he wasn't making much of a difference by only throwing back a few. The young man replied that he was making a difference for the ones he threw back. Oftentimes people of great skill or talent may not perceive that their contributions actually make a difference. I can assure you that Fred Ball and Dick Bond made a significant difference for the tens of thousands of vulnerable children and families affiliated with KVC.

I can also truly say that KVC was blessed with a wealth of quality board members. Many former board members offered not only wisdom and support but, in their own ways, worked to make life better for children in foster care. Both Dick and Fred were board members and were immensely special. They gave of their time freely, and each provided me with a quality sounding board. When growing an organization or business, there are always financial roadblocks and obstacles with which to contend. Rarely does someone in my position have the luxury of such talented advice givers.

About three years after I had moved to Kansas City to accept the CEO position at Wyandotte House, Inc and had begun expanding our services and our service catchment area, I encouraged the board to attempt something new. I wanted to create a campus. At this time in foster care nationally, children were being placed in multiple foster homes, shelters, group homes, and residential centers. As the saying went, "Come into foster care and see the state." In reality, many children in care not only got to see many foster homes in one state but placements in other states as well. Therefore, I wanted to create a center that would serve all the needs of a family so there would no longer be a need to move children from placement to placement.

In all of our years of service, property, and building expansion, Fred and Dick were always involved. More than anyone else not employed at our organization, they helped me to mold KVC into what it is today. Both accompanied me around the country as we asked one foundation after another for funding to ensure our success.

Fred was one who would ask me why I wanted to start a project. He wanted to hear about the vision; he wanted to know what the benefits would include from doing such a project and what the impact would be. He offered opinions on purchasing certain properties. He would explain his view on why one property would be better than another. Fred never said no to any of my projects, but in later years he did let me know that he wasn't fond of the vision of expansion outside of Kansas. As owner of Balls Food Stores, he often talked to me about how he liked his stores to be within driving distance so that he could randomly appear to check on each business site. During my tenure as CEO of this organization, I lived in two different locations within the metropolitan Kansas City area, and, in each location, I lived close to one of his stores. I would periodically bump into Fred while he was in one store or another, frequently on a holiday. I would have been sent by my wife to pick up an overlooked ingredient that was necessary for a large meal being made, and he would tell me that his wife, JoAnn, had sent him to the store for the same reason. While I knew that was possible, a more likely story was that he was popping into one store or another on the holiday to make sure the store was operating the way he wanted it to be operating.

Fred was hugely successful as a businessman. From my perspective, he was a very gracious and modest man. He knew humility even as he was growing a very large food business. There are some men who do not have to say much and yet people will follow and have great respect for them. Fred was one such man. Whenever I would call him, he would always make time for me. There are many successful men, but few would rival the sincerity and the wisdom that Fred possessed.

A favorite story of mine occurred on a very early trip Fred, Dick, and I took to meet with a major foundation. We were sitting on a plane and talking about our upcoming presentation, which we later perfected into a near science. I also talked to Fred about making a philanthropic gift. I said that we would need a major gift, and he responded that he was prepared to be a lead giver. He then asked what gift I wanted to receive from the foundation, and I said that I wanted to ask the foundation for a seven-figure gift, meaning $1 million. Without hesitation, Dick said to Fred, "Why don't you give a million?" Still looking at Fred, Dick added something to the effect that it would be great if we could say Fred was matching this potential foundation gift. Fred smiled and said that it seemed a little "strong" but possible.

During the actual foundation meeting, the person with whom we were meeting asked me about other major donors. I started mentioning a couple of significant pledges from Kansas City area foundations and businesses, when Dick hurriedly declared something like, "And Fred will pledge a million-dollar gift." The head of the foundation quickly looked at Fred and asked if that was true. Fred replied, "Yes." Then the foundation director turned to me and said, "Wayne, you better get that in writing." That gift was made over about a five-year period. And, yes, the foundation also gave us a million-dollar gift. This was the first time we had received seven-figure gifts, and, no, I never asked Fred to put his donation in writing. The generosity of Fred, and subsequently the entire Ball family, enabled KVC to create the highest level of services and have the latest IT equipment and facilities. Achievements like these made a tremendous difference in our recruitment efforts to ensure we were hiring the most capable staff and that we could retain them after being hired.

In the early 1980s, Fred and his family began a wonderful philanthropic event that grew from an annual party for food vendors in their backyard to what I believe became the largest charitable golf tournament in Kansas City. Gratefully, from the beginning of this Ball's Charity Golf Classic, KVC has been identified as the primary recipient of funds raised from this event. With Fred's passing, this annual tournament continues with his son, David, taking it to new heights. As CEO of Balls Food Stores and KVC's board chair, David continues his parents' legacy.

I will be forever grateful to Fred for many, many reasons, one of which was my introduction to another great person: Bill Self, the University of Kansas's men's basketball coach, not long after he accepted the job at KU. Fred would always (and his son, David, continues to) invite Coach Self to speak to the tournament sponsors for the Ball's Charity Golf Classic. Often, because our charity was linked to the tournament, I would also be asked to speak. After these events, I often stayed and talked to Bill. If you do not know Coach Self personally but have seen him on his television program or heard him speak at a function, I would say that what you see is what you get; he is one of the nicest, most personable individuals you could ever hope to meet. Invariably, Bill would ask, "Wayne, what can I do to help?" He always gave me the easy assist, and I did my best to get the proverbial slam dunk. Initially, he not only agreed to speak at the Ball's Charity Golf Classic, but also agreed to serve on our Board of Directors.

Knowing how badly we always needed new foster and adoptive families, I later asked him to tape some TV recruitment spots. He did so graciously and, as would be expected, phone calls came in after these segments were aired. In time, I also asked him to be the speaker at a fundraiser we were launching — the KVC Heroes Luncheon. With his participation, I think the very first year we raised nearly $40,000. Although an extremely busy person, Coach Self always stays after the luncheons to pose for pictures or sign autographs until almost everyone has left. With his annual commitment to this event, it has steadily grown, resulting in last year's (2016) donations reaching $200,000.

In our most recent capital campaign, Coach Self joined David Ball and me on a visit to a national foundation to request a cornerstone gift, and we were honored to be a successful recipient. There are all kinds of successful people in the world. Bill Self is one of those rare individuals who truly gives more than he takes and is the image of someone who pays good fortune forward. I cannot say enough good things about Coach (and KVC board member) Bill Self. He is truly genuine and deserves not only accolades for being a highly successful coach but for his conscientious efforts to improve the lives of thousands of children and youths.

Another great man who deserves recognition for all he's done for KVC is Dick Bond — someone I not only learned from but respected greatly. While Dick has always been very active in the community on a number of boards and advisory appointments, in his earlier work life he served in such diverse jobs as the first Overland Park city attorney, United States Congressional aide, state senator, president of the Kansas Senate, and banker. On any given day Dick was working on an array of different projects, all of significant merit. I first approached Dick in the early to mid-1980s. This was early in his career, but, clearly, he was a rising star in Kansas.

When I initially approached him to help me raise funds by co-chairing our capital campaign to build what is now our hospital and psychiatric residential treatment center, he was polite, he listened, and most importantly, he didn't throw me out of his office.

I probably got the largest laugh ever from him after he asked me how many meetings he would have to attend. Remembering that he had never heard of me and certainly not of our organization, which at that time was perhaps the smallest in Kansas but was now beginning to grow, I responded that I thought we would need about three meetings. I said this because I truly had no idea but didn't want to scare off a potential person who could really help. While that produced a hearty laugh at the time, I had no idea that I would hear my naïve comment repeated time and time again over the future years. Some things you can never live down.

Throughout the years, Dick Bond and I have visited and asked many different foundations and individuals for philanthropic support. No one has done more for KVC than Dick. We have met with individuals who indicated that they did not want to give money in Wyandotte County. We have met with foundations that did not want to give to our organization — thankfully not many. We have made multiple requests to a person who would not make eye contact while we were talking. We have been asked to kneel down on the floor with the head of a foundation, hold hands, and pray for the request. While we eventually got money from most of our contacts, I have to say the one request where we joined in prayer didn't result in a gift. I may have later accused Dick of not praying hard enough.

At the same time as our clinical staff members, led by Sherry Love, were seeking out researchers and the latest evidenced-based practices, we were dramatically assisted in our recruiting practices and our training capabilities by having the finest facilities, which allowed us to disseminate the latest research available to all of our urban and rural sites across multiple states. For this capability, I thank my friends Dick Bond and the late Fred Ball.

But Dick was more than a board member or a volunteer who helped me raise money for our KVC causes. He was (and is) a true friend. He felt deeply about our mission, and more than once he went out of his way to help make a difference for one of our foster children. During many Christmas Eve services at his church, he would request a special offering for one of our children in foster care who needed some special equipment or service. I also watched Dick as he provided loving guidance to a young adolescent who had been treated horribly by his family and others due to having a physical disability. To say Dick Bond is a special person would be as trite as saying we need water to live. He is simply one of the greatest men I have ever met.

# 6

# Wyandotte House: The First Decade

The development of the group home in Wyandotte County in the 1970s was consistent with the times nationally, and it was not without challenges. First, there was the constant need to hire strong husband-and-wife teams to serve as parents in each of these homes. Then, there was the difficulty in managing the finances and making the necessary reports to the state. Along with this came the challenge of trying to raise adolescents in group homes in the middle of urban neighborhoods. There were periodic, disruptive issues with neighbors that seemed to only worsen. The group homes were located in neighborhoods where families were beginning to move out and more transient populations or commercial businesses were beginning to move in.

Problems persisted, staff turnover increased, and it became more and more challenging to treat the youths referred to the organization. In fact, the youths' emotional and traumatic issues began to manifest in damages to the homes. The staff, without appropriate training, did not always take the necessary actions to avert erupting concerns, and soon the founding women began to seek additional support. Their initial efforts to hire professionals did not prove effective. In a short time, two homes became empty, and the third home dropped to only five children. With the diverse challenges that the fledging organization was facing, the ladies began to look for professional staff to provide operational leadership.

# 7

# My Introduction to Wyandotte House

With two young children in 1980, my wife and I wanted to return to the Kansas City area so my daughters could get to know their grandparents and extended family. This was further motivated when my father suffered a very serious heart attack; I wanted to be nearer very quickly. I began watching for opportunities for an executive director position in Kansas City, as did my mother. Given the financial climate in the '80s these opportunities were very limited. In fact, the executive director position at Wyandotte House was the only such position posted over a several-week period.

For all practical purposes, I was offered the position while in the interview, but I did have to wait for an official phone call. I was 33 years old at the time, and while I was very appreciative, I had some reservations given the organization's status. These reservations were overcome, however, by the members of the board who hired me. They were clearly an accomplished group of community business leaders and volunteers who had the children's best interests in mind. Although they had hired me due to my past work experiences, I had never worked in a group home and knew nothing about group home-type services. To be honest, the more I learned about the group home model, the less I liked about it.

The board chairman, Pete Pomerenke, was a successful businessman and also president of the local school board. In addition to all of his business and other civic responsibilities, he was trying to run this group home organization until a person could be hired, which proved to be problematic. This organization had been operating for a decade with mixed success. Initially, and for the first five years, the organization struggled but continued to grow. However, over the next few years it had begun a tremendous reversal, and so there was discussion around closing the organization.

After I was hired and had moved to Kansas City, the first couple of board meetings still included discussions about closing the group home doors. By then I had actually seen the workings of the one remaining operational group home, and I was in agreement that closing it might be the best option. For example, during my first week, I was asked by Pete to go with him to be introduced to the director and other leadership of the Regional Social and Rehabilitation Services (SRS) office (currently the Kansas Department for Children and Families). As we were getting off the elevator and were about 20 feet from the director's office, Pete turned to me and said that the other reason we were there was to talk about a sexual abuse charge made by a female resident against a Wyandotte House employee. I suspect this late revelation was to ensure that I would actually go to the meeting.

The meeting was interesting and very telling. I listened to a number of other concerns they had with our group home. While a bit sickened to my stomach after hearing about the sexual abuse charge and all of their concerns, I assured them that changes were coming. The next day, I met with each employee individually, and, from that day through the next few weeks, I replaced all of them.

Within the first two years of my employment, we reopened the two previously closed group homes and actually added another. The new home came about after a merger of sorts with another organization that was closing. The new home had been a federally funded home for runaway youths. The only problem was that there were no youths in the facility. As I watched, I saw that there was never more than one youth residing there at any one time. There were, however, always several employees present.

At the time that we were about to acquire this home, children in the foster care system were frequently moved to different foster homes or other group homes because there were no temporary shelters in the area to keep the foster children near their families until a more permanent solution became available. Prior to closing on this runaway program facility, I contacted the SRS regional administrator about opening an emergency shelter. The shelter would allow for youths to be placed temporarily while the state's case managers looked for a more permanent setting. The emergency shelter license was granted, and we combined the temporary shelter with the home for runaway youths.

While the runaway facility had almost always been empty, combining both programs into one created new referral sources and caused it to be filled from the first week. It also allowed for a more diversified funding stream. This was not rocket science; it was simply reading the environment and interpreting a better, more efficient, and more efficacious manner of addressing industrywide problems. Later in our history, based on additional learning and creation of new community-based services, we were able to eliminate or significantly downsize our use of emergency shelters but, at this juncture in our organizational growth, it was a monumental step forward.

At the time, I needed to make some decisions regarding personnel to operate the new facility. I terminated the employment of all of the full-time staff at the shelter and replaced the director with an intern working there who was just completing his undergraduate degree in social work from Avila University. After interviewing all of the staff who had either a graduate or an undergraduate degree, I found the intern to be the only one with the right values. That intern, Clarence Small, after working many more years with KVC, eventually left for a federal opportunity but remains active today as a foster/adoptive parent; he also volunteers with our chaplain in offering religious services for our inpatient populations. Clearly, the intern was the right choice.

So in coming to KVC, it was quickly apparent to me that to make this nonprofit work both programmatically and financially, I had to be a constant learner. The learning curve was rather steep and filled with some rather deep potholes that had to be averted. I knew that if we were to be successful, I was going to need to be very tenacious. I began reading about people who had achieved success in various professions and how, very often, those individuals had to overcome significant obstacles. Somewhere along this journey, I remember reading about the struggles and many failures of Abraham Lincoln, the 16th president of the United States.

Mr. Lincoln had a very challenging learning curve to say the least. He failed in two business ventures. His fiancée died. He suffered a nervous breakdown. He tried running for public office several times and lost most of them. However, after only winning one term in Congress, he was elected president of the United States. But that one election changed the face of who could be considered a United States citizen.

This was a wonderful model for all types of businesses. For me, it became a model as I often talked about changing the face of foster care. To me that meant doing what I could to change the way the foster care system functioned, including not allowing children to grow up in a state's custody, which unfortunately was the rule and not the exception. I have attended too many graduations of youths who spent their entire childhoods in state custody and had no true family to celebrate with them.

One example of a challenge I faced not long after I arrived involved a young woman who served as a house parent. We had given up on trying to hire only couples to provide this role because they were becoming impossible to recruit.

At that time, the house parents lived in a group home for four nights and were off for three nights. Their job was to serve as surrogate parents. These were generally bachelor-level individuals who were to provide supervision, meals, transportation, and parental-type counseling and to coordinate and approve entertainment. Group homes were not set up to provide any actual therapeutic treatment. For that service, a house parent would transport a youth to the local mental health center, a program practice I modified greatly in the years that followed.

The incident occurred after I had just purchased a side of beef because I wanted youths in our homes to eat well while in our care, and it was a very cost-effective way to feed so many. One afternoon, when I made an unannounced visit to one of our group homes, I found a large grocery sack with a purse lying immediately next to it. Out of curiosity, I looked to see what was in the sack. I found frozen steaks and frozen hamburger. A young female houseparent admitted to filling the sack with meat to take to her apartment for personal use. Needless to say, this young woman lost her job that day.

I had not thought anymore about the incident until one day when I received a phone call from the United Way (UW) office asking me to come to a meeting. As I was trying to learn how to fundraise, I had earlier applied and was accepted for UW funding. (In a later chapter I will expand on our fundraising.) Upon arriving at the UW office, I was ushered into a meeting room where I noticed a man sitting at a table; next to him sat the young lady I had terminated.

I was asked to take a seat, followed by the executive director of the UW, who began explaining the reason for the meeting. Apparently, the man sitting at the table was the father of the young woman and was also a minister at a local church. They then outlined the allegations against me and my organization. I was told that I was not providing proper care to the youths at the group home. The man mentioned that the youths were allowed to go to the local mall unattended, they were allowed to stay out late at a local state park, and they frequently were allowed to watch R-rated movies that had been checked out at a nearby movie rental business. (This preceded the Internet and downloading of movies.)

Based on these allegations, the minister and his daughter wanted to close down the organization. I really could not believe what I was hearing. I then mentioned that I had not read anything pertaining to such accounts in the logbook that recorded their weekly activities. By then, I had become more than a little angry, and, using my deepest, most agitated voice, I said the next thing I was going to do was to go to the district attorney's office and file criminal charges against his daughter for theft, negligence, and child endangerment. She knew her responsibilities, and in front of this group of people she admitted to these actions. I said I would be happy to show him the job description his daughter agreed to and the form she signed when she was hired. I mentioned that it included providing parental supervision on all outings, and among other items, specifically identified that no R-rated movies were to be shown. And I mentioned that only staff members had the card to check out movies at the rental store, so his daughter had to have checked out the R-rated movies.

The meeting immediately took a decidedly different tone. The father, then clearly flustered, stood up and said that he had never been talked to in that manner before and that while they were going to end their quest against our organization, he still did not think much of the group home where his daughter had worked. I continued my undaunted glare at him until he left. After that occasion, I had a particularly close relationship with the executive director of the United Way, who had appreciation for doing the right thing.

There were other daunting problems as well. When I started at KVC, most non-profits were struggling. Federal funds were being cut back as Congress was trying to balance a national budget. In fact, about five children's organizations in Kansas, as I recall, closed their doors not long after I arrived at KVC in 1980. It was a time of political turmoil internationally. Locally, I faced considerable turmoil as well.

But, while a number of non-profit organizations were closing their doors and federal funding was more than a little tight, our organization began to prosper by providing more diverse services and improving the quality of those services. Diverse services were needed to meet the needs of this population of children and families. It was at that time I began using what became one of our isms: *If we aren't growing as an organization, we are dying as an organization.* By this, I meant growth in any number of ways: quality, size, diversity, education, or complexity.

---

♥ KVC-ism

### *If we aren't growing as an organization, we are dying as an organization.*

---

I have mentioned this before, but it bears repeating. I had never worked in a group home organization and had never had a good opinion about them. But, definitely after I had begun in this position, I knew I didn't like group home-type programming. Group home licensure and funding did not cover therapeutic, medical, or education services and made it difficult to hire and supervise quality staff who shared the vision. By now, though, we had grown to four homes.

Another early example of a nonfunctioning group home model came after I began questioning the monthly gasoline bill. Early in my tenure, I found paying bills was a difficult challenge. There were times when

I would call the SRS Central Office requesting that I be allowed to come to Topeka to pick up the reimbursement checks owed to us. I did this because waiting for them to be mailed would have prevented me from making payroll. When I first came to KVC, there were five children in one group home. Our annual budget was around $200,000. The group home was old and needed many repairs. The staff members, small in number, were not very competent or trustworthy. Our reputation was almost non-existent. I struggled to make payroll and many times had to ride "the float," as bankers might say, meaning that bills were paid in hopes that the money would be in the bank by the time our checks were presented to be paid by the bank.

The state social services agency provided reimbursements for the placements they made to private organizations like KVC. SRS issued and mailed checks on a monthly basis to KVC. As mentioned before, on several occasions I had to arrange to go to Topeka on a Friday to pick up these checks. I would then have to drive back to the bank to make the deposits so there would be enough money in the bank to meet payroll. In the early days, I had to be the accounting department. I met with and admitted all new youths being placed and then completed the required state paperwork. I also did therapy with the residents, and, if they had parents, would provide family therapy. Initially, I was the plumber, painter, and general handyman for everything that needed to be done to keep the house running. Those who knew me well understood just how funny that really was. Later, as we began to grow, there were other wonderful staff members who helped me with these tasks.

Funding during this time was very restricted. So, when I began noticing a spike in gasoline bills, I began questioning the cause. Initially, I was told that the expenses were increased due to more youths having to be transported to the mental health center for therapy and more trips being needed to clinics for medical care. Not being satisfied, I went to the station that allowed our staff to charge gasoline to fill our organization's vans. At the end of each month I would approve payment to the station. When I followed up with the station owner, I found that several of our group home staff members were also filling up their personal vehicles in addition to our vans.

---

♥ KVC-ism

## *What would you want if this were your child?*

---

Early on, it seemed as if I was constantly terminating some staff member's employment. However, it soon became known that inappropriate behaviors would not be tolerated. At each hiring opportunity, I made a point to hire up. With every staff opening I began looking beyond college degrees to character, experiences, and matching values. I looked for individuals who shared our vision of what a foster care system could be. To help drive the change that we wanted, we began using the ism *What would you want if this were your child?* I took very seriously the definition of "in loco parentis," which means standing in the place of parents who couldn't be present or for whom rights had been terminated.

# 8

# Creating a New Vision and Culture

I became more and more determined to move away from the group home concept. My vision was to create a continuum of services that would meet all needs that youths and their families might have—one stop shopping, if you will—resulting in no longer sending children and families around the state or outside of it in order to get the services they need. Again, remembering my earlier experience, I was trying to merge the services of an inpatient facility with behavioral healthcare outpatient and other community-based services.

As we began to grow, I knew that it was imperative to have a good vision and a good mission if we were to be able to develop a quality organization. Both the vision and the mission had to resonate with our staff members. Culture is all about getting buy-in on a worthwhile endeavor first from staff members and then from the families with whom they are working. Clearly, improving the lives of children and their families was worthwhile, but all of the interactions between staff and families had to be authentic. All staff member interactions had to move the mission forward. It may sound relatively easy, but of course nothing worth having comes easily, at least not to me. However, over time as story after story of how our staff members were truly helping to enhance the lives of children began to be repeated and subsequently were told to new staff being hired, a culture with character began to emerge.

In the early 1990s, I hired our first full-time psychiatrist. We then began increasing services being provided within our own organization. This also dramatically increased our referrals. Then I began recruitment of a pediatrician to make sure the children and youths referred to us, many of whom had never had a physical examination, received prompt, proper medical care. Over the years our medical staff has diagnosed many previously undetected illnesses — some that were life threatening. We were able to serve many young people who otherwise would have been left without treatment.

---

## "Everything you are comes from your choices."

— Jeff Bezos —

---

We staffed with a full complement of medical staff, and we brought whatever services were needed to the youths. We made the deliberate decision to not send any youth away. Some examples of raising the treatment bar included treating youths with severe cases of pica, suicidal cancer patients, and pregnant teens determined to harm themselves. They each had value, but in the moments of their individual trauma it was hard for them to realize their worth.

Most non-profit organizations can provide good services if they have a good mission and a strong vision and are intent on exceeding expectations in quality. Look at the non-profit organizations in your community. The key is to be able to demonstrate how you differentiate your services from similar organizations and how you set yourself apart through quality services.

When I first came to KVC and we were only a group home organization, there were a total of four organizations in Kansas City, Kansas, that were offering basically the same type of services. Within three years, two organizations closed their doors, and the third was limited to only a fraction of the services it had been providing. KVC had usurped almost all of the referrals. These were not bad organizations, but beyond the national fiscal environment they also hadn't changed or grown programmatically. Providing the same services every year in the same fashion but without any detectable improvements is never the answer; it becomes part of the problem. Jeff Bezos said it like this: "Everything you are comes from your choices."

---

## "The remarkable thing is that we have a choice every day regarding the attitude we will embrace that day and every day."

— Charles Swindoll —

---

Charles Swindoll said, "The remarkable thing is that we have a choice every day regarding the attitude we will embrace that day and every day." At KVC, we paraphrased Aristotle (as well as Charles Swindoll), creating a new ism: *Excellence is not an act; it's a habit.* As non-profit leaders, we know that we and our staff members must make the choice as to how we will conduct business each and every day.

---

♥ KVC-ism

## *Excellence is not an act; it's a habit.*

---

I wanted to create a culture that encouraged each of our leaders throughout the network to model the behavior they wanted to see in others and to provide training that would position our staff members to be the best professionally and attitudinally in the country. Abraham Lincoln said that the best way to predict the future was to create it. KVC makes a habit of helping individuals to create the futures they want.

We know there are more than 11 million people — more than 10 percent of our American workforce — who work in the non-profit sector. In my work history with a state institution and community mental health center and as the CEO of a large non-profit behavioral healthcare organization, I have had the opportunity to work with numerous non-profit organizations and governmental agencies across the nation. What I have seen too frequently in too many entities is an abundance of complacency and adherence to the status quo.

Change in any activity is inevitable, but it does not guarantee improved organizational productivity or advancement of the mission. To enhance the charitable purpose requires a majority of the workforce to buy into the mission, vision, and culture of that organization and to persevere in growing and improving the methodology driving them. The charitable purpose may remain the same, but the service quality, training, and technology should be continually improving.

KVC was built on the following premise: Hire and retain the best people with the right values, train them in our culture, and factor in flexibility along with a willingness for some calculated risk and growth.

I wanted to create a culture built on values. I wanted our staff members and those who used our services to see that we truly wanted to improve their existence. We began by asking a simple question: "What would you want if this foster child were your child?" By making the imagery more personal, we removed the third-party mentality commonly heard in staff meetings across the country.

So we would say that if this were our child, then we would not want our child to be moved to multiple foster homes and group homes. We would want our child to be at home with us or, if that was impossible at the time, in another loving home, ideally a relative's. We would not want our child sent away to live in some distant group home far from friends and family. We wanted to maintain consistency. We wanted children and their family members to trust that we were not overlooking their wants and feelings. We also wanted to show respect to the mothers and fathers of children referred to us by fully including them in the planning process and making sure their voices were heard. Too often, they were relegated to the back of the room, behind the "professionals."

We felt that children needed a family to grow up in, and a group home did not qualify as a family. We were not supportive of long-term foster care. We believed then and we still believe that children grow best in families. Children were being maintained in foster care for years and years, and in fact many spent their entire childhoods in custody.

We began talking about "child time." This to us meant that there should be a sense of urgency about the child growing up in a permanent home. Growing up in a family was important, so decisions had to be made timelier. These were typical of the value statements we developed in order to teach our culture and what we expected from those who wanted to make a career at KVC.

I also wanted to drive a culture of growth and continual improvement. In this field and in the field of nonprofits in general, growth doesn't come naturally. Young behavioral healthcare or social work staff members are not emerging from college thinking about how to help a company grow but rather how to provide a certain skillset. Of course, these are not mutually exclusive. You should provide good skills if you want to grow, but the mindset must be different. I focused attention on continual growth. Growth in a company is exceedingly important for a number of reasons. Growth creates a healthier environment, and it generally helps the organization financially. It creates new and diverse opportunities for existing and new employees. It allows a company to not put all of its eggs in one basket. And it fosters an atmosphere for continual learning and continual improvement.

Every year, I encouraged my leadership to understand that we needed to expand in some capacity; that could include, among other options, new training. I felt we needed to be continually expanding an existing service or adding a new program. It was important to me that we drive an attitude of continual learning and growth. As an entity, if you are not growing, you are dying.

In the early years, we added a lot of new programs. These weren't particularly big programs, but they all moved our organization forward. We never chased grant-funded programs unless they directly tied into one of our existing core services or helped us fill an identified service gap that expanded the continuum of care.

Other organizations routinely chased grant funding, but when the program funding ended, they stopped the service and terminated their employees. When we had a grant-funded program that lost funding, we kept the employees who best understood our culture and who helped move our company forward. While other organizations focused on hiring individuals with certain degrees, or on hiring replicas, I focused more on hiring individuals who shared our values. I felt then and now that you can teach skills but you cannot always teach values or force individuals to buy into a culture. I also wanted to hire to our weaknesses and not hire those who demonstrated similar skills as we already possessed.

In my opinion, nothing happens by chance. Preparation and hard work are always the answer. To have a great team means, first of all, that team members must understand their responsibilities in the organization. They need to understand the mission of the organization. If the mission does not resonate with an employee, then it is better for all concerned to not have that individual as an employee. Then you need a great vision so all of the employees can see where the organization is headed and believe they can be a part of it.

I was and still am a fan of business consultant Jim Collins. I agreed with his comments about getting the right people on the bus and then getting them in the right seats on the bus. Several years ago, I remember doing a two-hour training on our culture for all of my employees. I included a segment on Jim Collins and his views on getting and keeping the right employees. Following the training, a longtime employee, Rev. Dr. Jackie Suttington, actually gave me a large model of a bus. On the outside of the bus was a sign that read "KVC Employees." From that day on, I displayed that bus prominently in my office as an outward reminder of my belief.

One reason why so many nonprofits are functionally irrelevant is that, too often, agency and board leaders focus too much on process and not enough on cultural development and on achieving outcomes. Too much focus is placed on how to maintain current services (the status quo) and a break-even budget. There are many reasons for this phenomenon, such as not wanting to have major problems during one's tenure as an organization leader or board member. Some may feel that maintaining the status quo or not rocking the boat is preferable to creating a culture of taking some risks in order to raise the service bar. But this, too often, indirectly produces a culture of honoring the status quo.

Often, there is an intense fear of risk. Of course, you cannot continually lose money, but playing it safe is not the answer to impacting the mission. Rarely is there a focus on what could be done to make a real impact on the non-profit mission, and few leaders look to establish a vision that produces quality services and continual growth. Again, I will repeat one of our isms: If you're not growing, you're dying as an organization. Each year we focused on growing our services and delivering quality outcomes.

Often the concern is fear of failure. As Elbert Hubbard said, "The greatest mistake you can make in life is to be continually fearing you will make one." Too much time is focused on mediocrity and the status quo and then feeling accomplishment when an organization stays between the lines and does not reach for goals that raise the service bar. In my opinion, this has been the typical case of nonprofits working with children in foster care. Of course, this phenomenon occurs in other nonprofits as well. For example, take a look at the non-profit organizations in any community over a five-year period and see how many have made any substantial growth.

---

## "The greatest mistake you can make in life is to be continually fearing you will make one."

— Elbert Hubbard —

---

That's not to say that growth should be the only way to judge an organization. Clearly, quality outcomes that truly measure aspects of the mission are the best way to assess the success of an organization. However, growth is the very best way to spread the mission. Others may feel the best way to judge an organization is by the size of an endowment. Many non-profit administrators and board members feel a sense of accomplishment offering the same service every year but having a substantial endowment. It would be similar to the adage of having 10 years of experience or one year of experience 10 times. In my opinion, a vision that expands the mission and maintains substantial reserves is the ideal — although rarely do these concepts run in tandem, especially if the nonprofits function primarily on governmental funding. Growth of any corporation, whether non-profit or for-profit, is very hard work.

In the case of my boards, even in difficult times, I was lucky to have found immense support. I received an abundance of encouragement. During my 35 years with KVC, some challenges occurred, generally over fiduciary matters. It was certainly understandable, especially in an organization that was growing rapidly. But these challenging times were extremely rare and of short duration.

# 9

# Investment in the Future:
# Philanthropy

Success breeds more success. It also breeds confidence, but neither occurs without being willing to try to tackle new areas in which you are not comfortable. Eleanor Roosevelt said it like this: "You must do the thing you think you cannot do." In the early years, philanthropy definitely fell into that category for me. But for a small non-profit organization, learning how to raise funds is definitely a must for most to survive. Receiving grants from philanthropic foundations underscored our early successes by actually helping to validate our non-profit organization's mission. I personally felt that in Kansas City if the Hall Family Foundation — the largest and most respected at the time — believed our organization was worthy of a major grant, then we had received the stamp of approval as a significant entity that was large enough to be recognized.

---

### "You must do the thing you think you cannot do."

— Eleanor Roosevelt —

---

Starting with a handful of children in one group home, it became obvious very quickly that the reimbursements we were receiving for each youth placed in our care were not sufficient to sustain our organization. In fact, we could barely pay staff beyond the very minimum. Certainly, this would not allow us to hire and retain quality staff, which was key to providing quality services.

In the first two years, we were able to more than double the size of our organization. Actually, we doubled or nearly doubled our size each year for the first five years. By then, we were becoming known and had reached the radar screen of the leadership of the SRS central office in Topeka. While this service expansion helped a little with budget flexibility, it was still nowhere near where we needed to be to effect positive change in our field.

My previous experience working in a state institution and a mental health center hadn't required raising funds privately like running a nonprofit does. State institutions and mental health centers receive funding either totally from the state and federal coffers or, in the case of mental health centers, partial funding may be provided through the counties they serve. Additional funding comes with the opportunity to bill federal and state matched funds from Medicaid through special billing codes that are not available to other providers.

I certainly knew of the United Way and had contributed in my prior jobs, but I was not knowledgeable about becoming a recipient. But I knew most reputable non-profit organizations were United Way agencies. Therefore, I was determined to become a member agency for the added funding and so that we could post the United Way insignia on our letterhead. Like anything else in life, not knowing about something is only the beginning of a new learning curve. Our work with philanthropy began with the United Way.

I decided to call and make an appointment with the executive director of United Way in Wyandotte County, a woman by the name of Annette Thurston. She was a very take-charge woman and ruled the recipient organizations with an iron hand. At the time Margaret Thatcher was prime minister of Great Britain and carried the nickname of the "Iron Lady." I always felt that handle could easily have applied to Annette. I remember attending a large celebratory luncheon one year after the United Way's financial goal had been reached and not long after we had been given recipient status. Annette asked the recipient organizational directors to stand as she called their names. I assume this was to allow others in the audience to recognize the leaders of the organizations benefitting from the funds raised by the community.

As Annette began calling each director's name, it became apparent that about half of the directors weren't there. The more names she called, the more her face reddened. I can't say I had perfect attendance at the regular United Way meetings, but I was certainly happy I was present for that luncheon. After she concluded calling all the names, she paused, looked around the room at those of us standing, and said, "I know which organizations will be getting less money this year." As I said, she could easily have carried the nickname of the "Iron Lady."

Years later, I was honored by her son when he called me to ask if I would serve as a pallbearer at Annette's funeral. He said that his mom had always respected me and had listed me as someone she wanted as a pallbearer.

But, I'm getting ahead of the story. My first meeting with Annette was only partially successful. Gratefully, she agreed to meet me, but the only group that would have been less happy to meet me would have been the existing organizational recipients. Annette knew that in Wyandotte County, while the annual fundraising goal was usually met, generally the goal remained pretty much the same year after year. This, of course, meant that each new recipient needed to share in the communal funding pot, which for years remained relatively flat, resulting in less for others.

Annette was businesslike. She was cordial but informed me that there would be a rather substantial waiting period before our organization could attain full recipient status. I believe it was about two years. Until then, we could receive about $2,500 a year and could list the United Way insignia on our letterhead. So, while we were not completely members at that time, we had charted a clear path. I rather happily mentioned to our board that our organization was now a provisional member. It seemed that in the early part of my tenure at KVC, I was always seeking validation and credibility in a field that continually maintained the status quo.

In similar fashion, I was welcomed with something less than a hearty pat on the back as I ventured into the foundation world in Kansas City, Missouri. As you may know, Kansas City, Kansas, is separated from Kansas City, Missouri, by a bridge; tourists literally can drive from one city to the other without knowing they have left one state and entered another. However, if you live in one, you definitely know the difference. At that time Kansas City, Kansas, was definitely the "Cousin Eddie" of the family. Today, Kansas City, Kansas, has transformed itself into the entertainment capital of Kansas and is prospering, but in the early 1980s it was a very impoverished city.

I knew nothing about the Missouri foundations but was determined to learn. The first couple of foundation representatives I went to see told me that their foundations did not give money in Wyandotte County. I was told their funds had been acquired by individuals and companies residing on the Missouri side of the line. This was a very straightforward approach to being turned down.

One trust administrator actually cursed at my unabashed attempt to get grant funds from him. I was more than a little frustrated, and a less determined person probably would have, or perhaps should have, given up.

It was not until the Hall Family Foundation partially opened the door to funding for our organization that we actually broke through to receiving foundation funds. We had gone to them in search of support to build our first treatment center. This would have been around 1984. Bill Hall, their foundation administrator, indicated that before he would make a grant to us he wanted to see the results of a feasibility study. So, initially, no grant was made to us, but the foundation provided an organization $13,000 to help determine if it was feasible for us to raise $1.2 million. Again, since funding really didn't cross state lines, the firm conducting the feasibility study began contacting only businesses and individuals in Kansas City, Kansas.

The feasibility study lasted about two weeks. One afternoon toward the end of the two weeks, the gentleman conducting the study asked to see me. He walked into my office and said he had some bad news for me. Before he could finish his sentence, I told him I had to leave for a meeting but asked if he was available for dinner that evening. We met at the Plaza III restaurant. Over dinner, he told me that the people in our county thought well of our organization but that no organization from the county had ever been able to raise that amount of money.

I asked if those interviewed had suggested an amount we might be able to raise. He said it was believed that we could raise about $400,000. Without hesitation, I said that we planned a campaign of three phases of $400,000 each and that I was so pleased he felt we could reach our goal. Instead of being sorry that we could not make our goal, we ended up having a celebratory dinner.

Ultimately, we didn't need three phases. We raised $1.5 million, which was well beyond our campaign goal of $1.2 million, in only about five months. I thank JoAnn Ball and Dick Bond, our co-chairs for that first capital campaign, for reaching our goal so quickly.

Winston Churchill said, "Success consists of going from one failure to another without losing enthusiasm." That statement truly represented our initial efforts at raising funds privately. Much credit, again, has to be given to Dick Bond and JoAnn and Fred Ball and their entire family for believing in our mission and vision and then working hard to reach fruition.

---

## "Success consists of going from one failure to another without losing enthusiasm."

— Winston Churchill —

---

Once we had begun our upward trajectory, we were rarely turned down by the foundation community. Prior to making an official grant request, I started inviting personnel from foundations to visit KVC so I could introduce them to our organization and begin laying the groundwork for a grant request. Remember, we were very small at this time, and few had heard of us. We were located in downtown Kansas City, Kansas. Across the street from our location was an apartment complex where most of the tenants were unemployed and often found sitting on a sofa under a tree directly across from our entrance. From early in the morning until late in the evening, many could be observed drinking beer. Our guests included many notable dignitaries such as Adele Hall, Esther Sunderland, and Barnett and Shirley Helzberg. While the neighborhood impression worried me somewhat, it did not appear to faze these wonderful philanthropic leaders. It may have only reinforced our community's needs, as we subsequently received support from these philanthropic leaders and from many others who followed their lead.

I truly believe that had we not received that original capital campaign grant from the Hall Family Foundation, we would never have been able to meet the funding target. Having a grant from the Hall Family Foundation was, and still is today, a stamp of approval for not only all of the Kansas City, Missouri, foundations but for several out-of-state foundations as well. We had finally arrived, as was subsequently demonstrated by support from national organizations, such as the J.E. and L.E. Mabee Foundation and The Kresge Foundation. In addition, it set the course for longstanding local support from entities including The Sunderland Foundation, Dunn Family Foundation, The H&R Block Foundation, and others too numerous to count. My introduction to Bill Dunn, Sr., in those earliest years also opened a door to what would become decades of mentorship for which I am very appreciative.

I do, however, remember a few notable rejections that took the air from my lungs. I would often ask board members or other community leaders to accompany me when meeting with a foundation. Prior to the meeting, I would explain to the person accompanying me how the process would work. I would describe that we had already laid the groundwork and that the foundation was very likely to give us a grant. And, I said, if we listened carefully we would be told if the foundation would fund us and roughly what monies we could expect to receive. I would mention that whatever the gift amount was, it would be important to thank them. I knew once we had established a relationship, we could prove ourselves and return later for larger amounts. Unfortunately, on occasion, the individual accompanying me would not retain that message, and in fact, would indicate that whatever amount a foundation representative suggested was not nearly enough. Obviously, on such occasions, we were turned down for any donation.

Raising funds for a small non-profit organization while competing for the same philanthropic dollars with hundreds or even thousands of other small non-profit organizations, not counting the major organizations and universities, requires a great mission with leaders and volunteers focused and following a plan. For any important meeting or negotiation, I quickly learned to take only the specific leaders/board members needed for very specific roles and to be certain each person is well suited and well prepared.

By raising philanthropic dollars, we were able to successfully complete numerous capital campaigns throughout the years. When combined with other fundraising efforts, these totaled approximately $20 million. Without using any state funding, we were able to build numerous facilities over the years of which any child, family, or staff member would be proud. This often went against the status quo in the not-for-profit world. It was another way in which we could show respect for our clients and staff and differentiate KVC as an organization. We built a new psychiatric hospital and opened another, with each including an adjoining psychiatric treatment center. We subsequently built a large conference center, outpatient program, office building, and corporate office complex that all had the latest technology equipment. In addition, the KVC Institute (which I'll discuss in a later chapter entitle Innovations Institute) became a reality due to philanthropic support. Truly, the ability for KVC to raise private philanthropic funds to enhance services to children and families also helped make us a national leader in child welfare and behavioral healthcare.

As a final thought on philanthropy and nonprofits, I often ponder the fact that the cost of fundraising or overhead is frequently challenged. While areas such as marketing, sales, and technology infrastructure are highly valued in the for-profit world as necessary for business growth and quality, the expectation by some is that nonprofits should not spend any money on fundraising or infrastructure. In my opinion, the focus should not be on what it costs to raise funds but on the return on the investment in relation to those costs. If the goal is for an organization to grow and serve more people, we must think beyond maintaining the status quo. We must think and act bigger. (There is an interesting TED Talk by Dan Palotta about this very thing.) Again, it's not what it costs you to raise money or to market your services, but rather the net return that allows you to improve your services and provide for more individuals. It is important, however, to keep your overhead as low as possible while still meeting your needs.

# 10

## Creating Our Prairie Ridge Campus

After I had been with KVC for some time and we had expanded to include additional community-based programs such as child-placing agency (foster family) and in-home therapy programs, I continued to notice that many children in foster care were being moved in and out of psychiatric hospitals. The closer I looked at where some of these mostly young adolescents were being admitted, the less satisfied I was with what I saw. I became convinced that there were really no effective psychiatric facilities for children and adolescents in the area. There were state psychiatric hospitals; free-standing, for-profit hospitals; and a number of area hospitals with psychiatric units that, in my opinion, were not meeting the needs of children in foster care.

As a general rule, these hospitals admitted both adolescent and adult patients into the same units. Neither I nor any of my team found this to be appropriate, but it was the customary practice at the time. I also found that once the children or youths were discharged from the hospitals, no residential treatment programs in the area were willing to accept them because their needs were too severe, too challenging, or too expensive.

This typically meant that these children might be sent across the state or out of state to some other facility that had a vacancy and was willing to admit them at a specialized rate. Even then, few facilities were willing to tolerate extreme behaviors. Thus, youths with serious emotional problems were moved repeatedly and placed in multiple treatment settings. Today, we know how much trauma that must have caused these boys and girls.

This frequency of moves would not have been tolerated by adults, but children and adolescents who had absolutely no control over any part of their existence were forced to accept their plight in life. The hand that these state wards had been dealt at birth moved them from what may be considered a potentially normal childhood to one that was nearly unbearable. Depression and unhappiness were common commodities among these youths. It was the behaviors these youths were exhibiting that drove the discharges without regard to the reasons for the behavior. Today, if you had the opportunity to walk into any prison in the country and poll the inmates, you would find that large numbers of prisoners had spent time in the foster care system in some state. It would be the same if the homeless population was to be surveyed. We knew we needed to stop this game of musical chairs being played with these children, always remembering my favorite ism: *What would you want if this were your child?*

Years later, through important studies, such as the Adverse Childhood Experiences Study (ACES), we learned more about trauma and the significant negative lifetime impact it has on children, and we embraced research as an opportunity to improve our services. KVC began focusing on the "why" of the behaviors and less on the actual behaviors and began looking for better research-based therapeutic approaches.

In the mid-1980s, however, as we were building our first treatment facility, we continued to observe this frequency of movement in and out of residential programs, and, after several of these placements failed, we watched the flow in and out of psychiatric hospitals. Many youths had escalated behaviors as a direct result of having been moved to a multitude of different placements. Often as a result, many foster youths became severely depressed and even attempted suicide. All over the country you could read about suicides of state custodial wards.

In approximately the same era, the concept of diagnostic related group-ings (DRGs) began being used. Generally, what this did was to stan-dardize lengths of hospital stays for a related group of medical diagnoses. For example, take the diagnosis of appendicitis. A patient with this diagnosis code would have funding approved for a two- or three-day stay in the hospital. Hospitals would no longer be paid if they chose to keep patients longer, regardless of the particular hospital policy for that surgery. However, psychiatric hospital admissions were not originally included in the establishment of DRGs. So what we began seeing were children and adolescents being admitted into psychiatric hospitals with pre-determined 30-day lengths of stays, matching what the insurance companies were paying at the time.

What was interesting was that on exactly the 30th day, KVC would often get a call from one of these psychiatric hospital units trying to place a sometimes psychiatrically unstable youth with KVC when the insur-ance money had run out. When those youths were admitted to KVC, rarely did we get a discharge summary with recommendations until weeks after the discharge. The psychiatric DRGs were eventually imple-mented, which meant the inpatient stays could no longer be 30 days but rather someplace between one and generally 10 days, depending on the diagnosis and the insurance company. It was then, over about the next 18 months, that most of the freestanding psychiatric hospitals closed. It was the same for many psychiatric beds in medical-surgical hospitals. These services were no longer financially viable enough to warrant keeping the units open. This is one of the major reasons for the shrinking number of inpatient psychiatric hospital beds and treatment facilities across the country.

On the verge of mental health reform across the country, the KVC board agreed that we should move forward with building a treatment facility and a psychiatric hospital. We first had to find property and then go through a series of public hearings to get the land zoned. Because KVC originated in Wyandotte County, Kansas, I began looking for a suitable property in the county. I believed that we needed a minimum of 40 acres to build the facility and to have enough space that we eventually could have such activities as an adventure course and appropriate recreational areas. (Why I felt 40 acres was necessary, I cannot really remember; I just know that I was adamant about needing 40 acres.) The process of acquiring and zoning the land took three years, but it seemed like 30. During this process, I was reminded of a comment Louis Pasteur had made, that his tenacity was the strength that led him to reach his goal.

I went to many zoning meetings with less-than-happy county residents. It was a very unpleasant experience, and, had I not been so stubborn or tenacious, I would probably have discontinued my search. Following many of these City Council meetings, I was walked to my car by angry potential neighbors who insisted on letting me know they were less than enchanted by my vision of creating a campus for children. I was turned down on multiple properties that I took to the City Council. During this time, my oldest daughter was a preschooler, and she loved to answer the phone when it rang. (At this time, we had telephone landlines; cell phones had not been invented.) I had to stop allowing my daughter, much to her dismay, from answering the phone because she was hearing language that was much too colorful and obscene for a four-year-old.

Eventually, Mayor Jack Reardon called me to his office and offered to help me zone a sufficiently large piece of property. I believe the eventual property ended up being somewhere between 50 and 60 acres. But first he asked me if I was going to continue to seek zoning on a piece of property. I said I was, and I remember saying to him something to the effect that he was the "city father" and that he should be concerned about "city children" without parents. I think he realized that I was resolute about the property. So, he told me to look at some properties that Kansas City, Kansas, owned and then come back to his office in a week to let him know which property I had chosen.

I very excitedly did as he had asked. However, when I returned with my favorite choice, he told me I could not have that one. He also told me I could not have my second through my sixth choices. When I got to my seventh and last choice, the mayor said he would help me get it zoned. Additionally, he indicated he would work with me on any financing we might need in order to install roads and bring utilities to the property. This, of course, was a tremendous opportunity.

I said, "You could have just had me go look at the one piece of property." He looked at me and laughed and replied, "I know." I think it may have been some payback for the long saga I had put him and the other council members through.

Later that year, my wife and I bumped into the mayor and his wife at the Junior League Ball. When I introduced my wife to the mayor, he said, "Are you really married to him? If you are, then God help you." This comment was good for a hearty laugh from all of us. It had been an unbelievably painful process, but it was over, and we could then laugh about it.

After the acquisition of the land, Dick Bond, the mayor, and I met several times, and gratefully, the mayor came to help us dedicate the initial building. I have to truly thank Mayor Reardon for his willingness to step up and help us find the necessary property. I also thank the Board of Public Utilities for the property and for assistance in bringing utilities to the site. Without this help, KVC may not have developed as we did.

During the process, I sought support from the commissioner of Social and Rehabilitation Services (SRS). I was overwhelmingly shocked to learn from the commissioner that he was totally against KVC building this new facility. In fact, his comment was that if we built the facility he would make sure no children were referred to us. I was very frustrated due to the obvious need and the fact that kids were continually being sent across Kansas and out of state for treatment services.

I explained that what we planned was a program that would accept any child or youth the state might refer to us and that the state would no longer need to send children out of state. There were no other programs like what we had planned; this would be a first. We envisioned creating a "no-reject, no-eject" treatment facility and psychiatric hospital. At the time of this discussion with the commissioner, there were multitudes of psychiatric hospital units discharging children (foster and other children) with little to no discharge documentation. Believing that we were right, I encouraged our board to move forward despite the commissioner's initial edict and to build the facility against his will.

Truly, this was a monumental risk. Our organization could not have recovered had the state withheld referrals from this setting. Graciously, the board followed my lead. Had they not supported me, I believe our growth would have significantly slowed, and we would not be where we are today. Actually, I doubt seriously that we would still be in business since our organization was so small. It should be noted, however, that before the building was completed the commissioner had reversed his position; in fact, he agreed to underwrite the cost of all of the beds for the first year whether or not they were occupied (and they were always occupied). Miracles do happen if you are willing to take the risk on what's important to make them happen.

As I had promised, we operated the residential treatment program with a "no-reject, no-eject" admissions policy, giving the area director of SRS decision-making authority on prioritizing referrals. From the beginning, this often meant serving children and youths that no other provider could or would serve due to their significant treatment needs.

As I've said, this was a time when young foster children throughout the country were often sent to other states for treatment purposes. There were always rationales for this, but none seemed to make much sense to me. Youths were generally sent out of state to a treatment center when no in-state organization would admit them. With literally hundreds of youths being sent out of state annually and paid for by either Medicaid funds or a state's general fund, it never seemed to make much sense financially or treatment-wise. And it certainly was unlikely to result in reunification of children with their families when they were far away and often unable to visit and participate in the treatment.

Sometimes an out-of-state placement might be the result of large residential organizations marketing directly to a judge or his/her subordinate staff members or state employees. Sometimes those facilities were part of a larger for-profit company that had programs in multiple states and was often dependent, in large part, upon referrals of youths in foster care from other states. This was the plight for many custodial youths from numerous states across America and unfortunately went on for many years.

With a strong marketing influence, often well-intended judges would order these placements out of state, and so children and adolescents would be sent away to be treated in isolation far from their families. Nothing could be done to prevent those placements, which often meant banishment, in some cases for years. As KVC began developing its own residential treatment programs and we'd hear of these instances, I or someone else would set up a visit to that out-of-state facility. I truly did this with the intent to learn from an organization that may have had better programming. What I routinely found was that, while the programs may have been held in high esteem by a particular court or group of professionals, the programs were often outdated, yet glamorized through effective marketing. I routinely found that a facility had never been visited by anyone in the court or state system, and so the referral status quo perpetuated. States rarely had the money to send a case manager to visit a facility, and the youth's family seldom had sufficient resources, so driven to despair the youth would likely succumb to believing that he/she was too challenging for anyone in the youth's own state and that he/she was without redeeming value. It is truly unfortunate that so many youths in the American foster care system were treated with such lack of civility. Whenever possible, whether it be in Kansas or out of state, I would seize every opportunity to talk with judges about this practice. Commonly, my first question was to ask if the judge had ever visited that facility. Invariably, the answer was, "No." I, on the other hand, had probably visited that facility and now had the ability to share my dismay about the inadequate service.

---

♥ KVC-ism

## *There is no magic answer down the street.*

---

The "grass is greener" phenomenon still has considerable draw in this field. In general, it's much easier and much less expensive to either not accept a youth with very challenging needs or to "eject" the youth from a program than it is to create and provide the best treatment. While there were times our visits to other facilities produced some learning of a particularly effective treatment practice or resource, more often than not we would return with the knowledge that we had more treatment capability for youths and their families. It was at this time that a new ism was created: *There is no magic answer down the street.* If we didn't have the capability, we had the commitment and willingness to find it and to bring services to the children and their families rather than send them away. We were constantly asking ourselves, "What more? What else?" These questions drove our appetite for education and research, bringing the application of evidence-based and/or best practices into routine programming throughout our programs. As our knowledge and skills grew, so did the positive outcomes for children and youths with the greatest of behavioral healthcare challenges.

Thankfully, the practice of sending youths to treatment facilities far from their families is rapidly becoming obsolete. Fewer and fewer states are sending foster youths to other states for treatment, and the use of residential services overall is decreasing. Instead, states are better using their financial resources to create community-based services to help keep families together whenever possible and are placing children with relatives or foster families far more often.

Building upon our continual advancement of inpatient practice, three years after opening our psychiatric residential treatment units, we expanded our initial building to officially create the hospital campus, including a younger children's emergency assessment unit. Dick Bond facilitated the assistance of United States Senators Bob Dole and Nancy Kassebaum and Representative Jan Meyers, who joined in to help raise the funds needed. Subsequently, we named a wing of the building after these elected leaders, and it was an extreme honor that all three came to the dedication.

During construction, I contacted The Joint Commission so we could design the building to their safety specifications for a children's psychiatric hospital. This too became a very interesting process. In the late 1980s and early 1990s, there were a number of psychiatric hospitals and several psychiatric units in area medical/surgical hospitals in Kansas, but none had been built exclusively to meet the unique needs of a children's psychiatric hospital.

Having been initially exempted from the DRGs, many of these other psychiatric programs were marketing to the state to have children and adolescents with Medicaid cards admitted to their facilities. This was a disturbing process and, at least in my belief, was one of the reasons the state of Kansas had a class action lawsuit brought against it for failing to provide adequate care to youths in foster care. The original suit, brought on behalf of an adolescent girl in state custody, identified recommendations made by a hospital and other groups regarding the treatment of this girl that, after months, had not been acted upon. In fact, hospitals were so uninformed about child welfare services that their service recommendations often didn't even exist. They were operating in isolation and with no ultimate responsibility.

Child welfare programming appeared to be stagnated. Many youths were being placed in one of the hospitals around the city or out of state. Discharge information was often limited and might take weeks to receive, which made planning very difficult and created gaps in services. Again, the recommended services often weren't even available.

During this time, I was working on an additional graduate degree in healthcare administration. In my graduate program, I began to focus on applications of Medicaid funding and how that funding was being used to pay for these hospital admissions. Upon my graduation and knowing how youths in the foster care program were bouncing in and out of hospitals, I focused on developing a new inpatient program.

I knew how many Kansas youths were being placed in area hospitals, how high the costs were, and, most importantly how these placements often resulted in fragmented care. Youths in foster care were cycling in and out of psychiatric programs. They were seeing different psychiatrists on each admission, which frequently meant a change in medication or, in many cases, simply adding on additional medications. Many of these youths, after their 30-day stay in the hospital, were then referred to our temporary emergency service program. This meant that the Medicaid or other funding had run out for this episode, but no relevant planning had been put together to accompany the youth. Although emergency/temporary shelters were not equipped with clinical staff, KVC was left to do the discharge planning that should have already been completed. Many of these young people's parents had had their parental rights severed, and the depression that followed could not simply be treated with more medication.

There was, in my opinion, little focus on getting foster youths reunited with their families, if possible, or on finding a forever family. The hospital programs were generally isolated entities interested in discerning a diagnosis, starting a drug regimen, and subsequently discharging to whatever bed was available in the system. There was also little to no connecting of the community treatment options following a discharge or for connecting the services to achieve the youths' safe return to their families.

KVC had a couple of psychiatrists and a pediatrician on staff at the time, and we rarely if ever referred anyone to an area hospital. Instead, operating under the "no-reject, no-eject" policy, we safely and effectively treated youths that others often would not, or could not, treat.

After putting my business plan on paper, I approached the commissioner of the Kansas Medical Services (Medicaid/Medicare) and shared my information and concerns. I also shared my cost calculations and information about how services and discharge summaries could be both timely and relevant to this population and to the foster care system. Personally, I thought the commissioner would not give me much time since he was in the midst of mental health reform, but he was more than excited about this opportunity. Also, much to my surprise, he asked for a second meeting to present to others in his department.

Afterwards, he enthusiastically endorsed the plan, and when he did he called together the executive directors of the area community mental health centers in a seven-county area nearest Kansas City and the administrators of area hospitals who had psychiatric units. The commissioner wanted me to present the concept to them, and it was truly a learning experience. Remember, at this time the DRGs were excluded, which meant that this was a very viable financial service for hospitals.

We ended up holding three meetings, which required many hours of preparation by me and Anne. They took place in 1991, just before our hospital was completed and opened. Despite this investment of time, the individuals to whom I presented either could not see the vision or possibly did not want to. I knew this was somewhat of an affront to them. After all, they were considered the area experts. Other hospital administrators were less vocal, but none were happy with our entrance into this service market.

During the third meeting, the head of the KU Psychiatric Department in 1991 summed up their concerns by asking, "How are you going to provide a psychiatric hospital program? Who are you going to get that's qualified to run such a program?" This was certainly meant to diminish our credibility. Clearly, he saw KVC as an upstart foster care organization to which he gave no credibility. I replied that I had a graduate degree in healthcare administration, and I was going to hire certain members from his graduating class of psychiatric residents. Of course, those were the ones who had, for all practical purposes, been running the KU psychiatric hospital program. I also mentioned that I was making the assumption that if they could graduate from the KU residency program in psychiatry and run the KU inpatient program they were undoubtedly competent enough to run mine. The meeting that began in such a contentious fashion ended far more agreeably.

KVC worked hard to build trust and expertise, and fortunately KVC and KU developed a close working relationship and now partner on a number of initiatives. As of this writing, KU fellows seeking credentials in child psychiatry complete their inpatient rotation at our hospital. An adult psychiatric inpatient unit has now been established on our Prairie Ridge campus with KU. Their partnership with us helped produce our tele-psychiatry program, which has been helpful in providing services to our rural areas. KU and KVC make for a great partnership that I believe will only expand and improve services throughout the state. The seeds for this professional collaboration were planted early and watered often.

One point I am trying to make in this chapter, which may not be very obvious, is that too often we as professionals in the field tend to perpetuate the status quo. Over the years I have heard many speak in different states of what needed to be done to address a well-known child welfare problem. Generally, their following comment had to do with blaming some other group like state employees for not doing their jobs or blaming insurance companies for the barriers they create. They might complain about kids cycling in and out of psychiatric hospitals with little results, or they might complain about a dozen or so other things. The bottom line is that less time is spent brainstorming solutions.

One of our isms is *Attack the problem, not the person.* You must be willing to identify barriers, and then you must do something differently to help resolve them. Too many people are totally enamored with the process of identifying problems as if that were the only goal. I used to tell our leadership that if they brought me a concern, they also needed to bring solution-oriented ideas. I also wanted them to be able to tell me what had previously been tried to improve the problem. Only then did we have a foundation for solving the problem together.

---

♥ KVC-ism

## *Attack the problem, not the person.*

---

Placing troubled children in and out of hospitals, changing medications or adding on more medications, and then discharging the children after the insurance had exhausted was a well-identified problem. The answer was to create something new.

We created a hospital program that did much more by involving families and, subsequent to their children being discharged, connecting them to our community services. We recommended precise discharge planning.

And if a child had been admitted with more than two medications in the same classification or if the child had been prescribed a medication dosage too high for our protocol, our physicians generally discontinued unnecessary medication or reduced existing dosages. But to accomplish this, we needed to have the resources, and we needed to be willing to stand up against those who were benefitting from the status quo. The beneficiaries of this answer, of course, were the children, who were pawns in a system that perpetuated doing the same thing.

In our earliest years of providing psychiatric hospital services, we served predominantly children who were in the foster care system, other state wards, and Medicaid-funded clients. Over the years, our growing expertise resulted in over half of our hospital census representing children from families throughout the community, supported by private insurance. Regardless of the referral source, our philosophy on the use of psychotropic medication has been consistent and is taken very seriously. We strongly evaluate the use of such medication upon a patient's entry to our hospitals and work to safely reduce the medication to the lowest degree possible. This medication should not be the only form of treatment but instead should only be given when necessary. Supportive therapies and other strategies should be acquired and integrated.

In later years, as we assumed responsibility for case management in foster care, we expanded upon this process for children in our care. Evaluation of medications begins during the admissions process and is followed up by the assigned case manager, who enters the information into our medication tracking software program. Inappropriate usage or dosage immediately triggers an automated email to a member of our medical staff, generally our medical director, indicating that existing prescribed medications exceed our protocols. This triggers one of our psychiatrists to contact the prescribing physician for additional background information. More often than not, this process results in a reassessment and reduction of medication. I have seen situations where young, small children have been prescribed psychotropic medications in a dosage that would be significant for a large adult. On occasion, we have had to send children to an area emergency room from our psychiatric hospital for medical stabilization due to overmedication before we can initiate treatment. Our protocol is an enormously important check and balance for children.

In 2003, about a decade after our psychiatric hospital opened and after our inpatient expertise and successful outcomes were well established, we approached the head of SRS about closing the state psychiatric hospital's doors to children and adolescents in Kansas City. Many discussions and four years later, KVC became the state contractor responsible for accepting all child and adolescent admissions that had previously been referred to the state hospital. By 2009, state hospitals across Kansas had closed their doors to admitting children and adolescents. KVC had opened an additional psychiatric hospital in Hays, Kansas, that along with our hospital in Kansas City could serve all children and adolescents statewide who were previously placed in a state hospital.

Another early development at our Prairie Ridge campus was our emergency children's assessment unit (CAU). Prior to this unit's development, standard practice was for police to take children who were being removed from their homes due to abuse or neglect to emergency foster families. Since foster families might have only one opening, this often meant a long evening filled with splitting up sibling groups during a time of extreme trauma. My vision for our CAU was to raise the level of service to include keeping all siblings together. While children were there, I wanted to not only provide a safe environment but to make sure the children were thoroughly assessed, received adequate nourishment, and had their health needs met. Many had never seen a doctor or dentist before and were in very poor health. With the pediatrician, nurses, and social work staff, we were able to fully assess and address children's needs prior to transitioning them to one of our community foster families because children grow best in families.

One evening police officers brought us 15 children who were all under the age of 10 and who represented two families. The mothers, who were sisters, were living together with their children in a drug house, and so the children were removed. When the police arrived with the children, the babies were in dirty diapers, many children were wearing filthy clothing and no shoes, and most of them had very bad cases of lice. Our nurse supervisor even felt the need to burn all of their clothing. This was late in the evening, and none of the children had eaten that day. Staff were pulled from all areas to fix food and to help bathe, clothe, and soothe these distraught children. While individually these characteristics were typical of the children we would see in this unit 24 hours a day and 365 days a year, collectively this represented the largest sibling/cousin group admitted at any one time. Once this unit was opened, it filled quickly and was well utilized. While some had doubted the need for this service or our ability to achieve the vision, following this event no one questioned our ability to respond to community needs.

In addition, by the time Prairie Ridge was fully developed, we had embraced the need for expanded community-based services such as in-home therapy, family preservation, adoption, and foster care. We had also created a partial hospital/day treatment program affiliated with the local school district. We had truly achieved my vision of a center that offered a full continuum of services for the region. The needs of any child or family referred could be met, from in-home therapy to supporting them in staying together safely to community foster care to inpatient hospitalization. Families no longer had to cross the state to access needed services.

With the consolidation of all of our inpatient treatment programs on this campus, we no longer needed our original group homes in downtown Kansas City. After considering various options, we felt the best utilization for these homes was to donate them to area families who had a history as foster parents with KVC. These large homes could then be licensed to accommodate a larger number of children in care, enabling these families to help us meet our goal of keeping sibling groups together.

It's relatively easy to look back on decisions like this and say that, of course, this made total sense and that it needed to be done. Jim Collins, the noted author of the *Good to Great* book series, speaks to how great organizations distinguish themselves from good ones. Oftentimes it means going against the established grain and being willing to provide solutions for the greatest challenges. I believe that we did that at KVC.

# 11

## Child Welfare: Early Perspective

According to the organization Child Help, every year there are more than 3.6 million referrals to child protection services agencies involving more than 6.6 million children. In fact, Child Help indicates that a report of child abuse is made every 10 seconds, and of these referrals 3.2 million are investigated. Reports are generally broken into categories of physical abuse, sexual abuse, emotional abuse and neglect, and physical neglect. In 2014, state agencies confirmed an estimated 702,000 victims encountered some type of child maltreatment.

This is a national tragedy and one that has to be systematically approached. For too long, children entered the foster care system and, in many cases, remained longer than necessary. The federal government's Child and Family Services Reviews are definitely a step forward in tackling areas where child welfare improvements are needed in each state. However, given state governments' need to balance budgets, maintain consistency with high leadership turnover, and handle the array of other more pressing state problems, child welfare often fell to a very low position on states' agendas.

It was challenging to look at the large state foster care program and say exactly where improvements were needed. Remember that when there was a referral every 10 seconds to child protective agencies and the media generally came in for high-profile cases, it was extremely hard to focus on specific areas of concern.

It must be remembered that the purpose of child welfare was to remove a child from his/her home in order to protect that child. If safety for a child is an issue, then the child should be placed in a safe setting. However, many times safety was not the reason children were removed or remained in the system. When safety was the reason for removal from the home, oftentimes the original safety issues that brought children into care were forgotten, while additional hoops to jump through to improve their well-being, such as health or education, were added. If getting poor grades was a precursor to entering the foster care system, I could imagine thousands more children in care.

Early in my tenure in Kansas, there was an enormous problem in assisting children either to safely return home or to be adopted in order to reach permanency, as is the vernacular in this field. Often, too many professionals were involved with each child and family — some with differing goals — resulting in fragmentation. It was not uncommon for multiple therapists to be involved with one family. While these professionals may have been providing good service, they were frequently working with a family without a unified treatment plan. It seemed like each professional had his/her own plan for eventual placement.

I used to hear my mother say when she was cooking a big meal for the extended family that "too many cooks spoil the broth." In this case, too many professionals participating with one family meant the outcome was likely to be delayed far too long, which meant the child would likely be placed in multiple foster homes and congregate care settings. This was further complicated when group home staff might have thought the child's behavior did not warrant visits or an eventual return to his/her home since, understandably, the child had probably begun to act out behaviorally.

System reform is good for many reasons, not the least of which is that reform efforts bring to light status quo issues in systems. Typically, these evolve from practices that were initially put in place and then over time became enshrined as best practices. When every part of the system is reviewed, every part of the system has to justify its reason for existence.

Foster parents were then and are still now the backbone of child welfare services. Without them, many more children would have to reside in congregate care settings and learn how to live in an institution instead of how to function in a family. Foster parents provide love and both emotional and physical nourishment to vulnerable children who, in many cases, have been severely abused.

In the 1970s and through the 1980s, foster parents were not allowed to, or at the very least were discouraged from, adopting children who had been placed in their care. This was considered a conflict of interest. Today that sounds foolish, but at the time that was the status quo. At KVC, we did not feel this was right, and so while the goal is family reunification whenever possible, we advocated for the right of foster parents to adopt children with whom they had bonded and loved and who could not be returned home safely.

It was believed by some that if foster parents were given the opportunity to adopt, then we would lose them as a foster family resource. Others believed that it would give the foster family an undue advantage over those not wanting to foster but still wanting to adopt. It was apparently thought that families who cared for a child, helped him with his school work, fed him, and went through the range of emotions with him should not have an advantage over another potential adoptive family. At that time, a child who may have been living with a foster family for months or even years was often moved once matched with an adoptive family. It's a blessing to have good adoptive resources for children, whatever the source. However, all children suffer from some level of trauma each time a significant life change, such as a change in placement, occurs. When a child who has suffered from the trauma of already being removed from at least one home is removed from yet another home to live with someone he or she may never have met, it can present great challenges. If a child has bonded with a family, not disrupting that placement may be the least traumatic and best option for that child. (Possible exceptions to this include when there is a relative already known to the child.) Again, system reform sheds light on status quo issues like this. It was not hard to see why so few children were adopted and why the failure rate for adopted children was so high in the foster care system during this era.

In the 1970s and 1980s, it was also considered good practice to allow and encourage long-term foster care. In the past, it was believed by many judges and state employees that long-term fostering was a better option than reunification or adoption. It was sometimes deemed inappropriate to rock the boat, especially when the foster parents were either unable or unwilling to adopt.

It seemed that undue burdens were sometimes placed on families wanting to adopt a child in the system. For example, I recall a family approaching me about adopting a three-year-old little boy whose parents had lost their parental rights and who was living with a KVC foster family that was unable to adopt him. Unfortunately, a job change took the family out of state, making them unable to adopt. I tried to intervene directly with the secretary of SRS, but I knew our conversation was over when he slammed down his phone. My frustration over this inane rule was compounded every time I saw this little boy in the future. The last time I saw him, he was around seven years old and was still in a foster home with no identified adoptive family. I suspect he spent many more years in that situation as long-term foster care was the general rule then.

More than once I pleaded my case to the secretary of SRS on adoptable children, only to be denied. Today, everything has changed. During the first couple of years of privatization, the number of foster children adopted doubled, and the rate continues to grow. Many more children now are finding forever homes with foster families who have loved and bonded with them. One of my favorite isms is *Children grow best in families.* Just because a practice has been a longstanding one — and it's the way we have always done it — does not mean the practice shouldn't be challenged.

---

♥ KVC-ism

## *Children grow best in families.*

---

Again, the practice at the time was long-term foster care. In many, perhaps most, areas of the country, it was the rule and not the exception. Long-term foster care might involve allowing a child to literally grow up in one foster home if lucky, or, as happened way too often, it might result in multiple foster homes and group home placements. Somehow, once a child entered foster care, it became very difficult for the child to get discharged from the system or to get adopted. That was what state administrators and many judges felt was best for the child who had been removed from a family considered to be undeserving or incapable of change. Everyone meant well and truly believed they were doing the right thing for children.

There have always been and probably will always be status quo issues like this that need to be challenged. But, for whatever reason, there is a continual reluctance to tackle these issues. Perhaps it's a fear to challenge state leadership or perhaps it's that many people simply walk through the motions of their jobs without fully considering the consequences. So, rather than focusing on foster children reuniting with a family or making sure there was a loving forever family, more attention was placed on supporting a long-term foster home placement because that was the way it had always been done.

Judges have a tremendously challenging job having to hear all of the information and then make fair and unbiased decisions. If you consider all of the input from child protective service workers and case managers, therapists, foster parents, court service officers, guardians ad litem, court-appointed special advocates, prosecuting attorneys, and parents' attorneys — coupled with the added continuances that attorneys often felt they needed — children could linger in a state's custody for years.

Well-meaning professionals often prolonged children's stays in foster care. An analogy might be made to the Eagles song "Hotel California": "You can check out any time you like, but you can never leave." All of these efforts frequently resulted in a child spending a large portion of his/her childhood in foster care.

Without children being returned home safely or being adopted, and with more children entering care, numbers in foster care were growing. This required more professionals to work with both children and families new to the system, in addition to the other children who had been in care for years.

A common dilemma in child welfare is that when the number of children in care increases, the focus understandably becomes more on playing musical chairs with resources to ensure that the child has a placement than on achieving permanency for the child. Due to these issues, the ACLU filed a lawsuit against the state of Kansas in 1989 for failing to provide adequate care to children in the state's foster care program. This ultimately resulted in a settlement agreement in 1993 with the Children's Rights organization. Little to no improvements in the 153 elements identified were made through 1995. By 2016, perhaps half of the states had experienced a class action lawsuit for many of the same reasons Kansas had been sued. Some of these states have been under a lawsuit settlement for over 20 years. Gratefully, Kansas exited the lawsuit settlement in 2001 after demonstrating significant improvement in all 153 elements.

# 12

## Winds of Change

In 1995, I was invited to attend a meeting in Washington, DC, along with four other CEOs from New York, Massachusetts, Wisconsin, and Texas. The invitation was from David Liederman, who was CEO of the Child Welfare League of America at that time. In the 1990s this was the leading association for child welfare organizations in America and Canada. David brought this group together to serve as a think tank to help him plan for the future in the field. (Eighteen years later I would be among seven CEOs from around the country to perform much the same function: to predict needs during the next decade. Only this time it was from the commissioner of the Administration of Children and Families in the Department of Health and Human Services in President Barack Obama's administration.)

David's questions were simple: "Do you believe managed care will come to child welfare, and if so, how soon do you think it will come?"

It was an interesting discussion and one that we pondered for some time. I had been sharing with my KVC leadership for years that I felt major change was coming. I had always tried to stay aware of significant cultural transitions in our region and nationally, and I shared my beliefs during our management team meetings and leadership retreats. During the late 1980s and early 1990s, I saw small independent store owners losing out to larger companies. Whether it was insurance agencies, pharmacies, or grocery stores, small private businesses were being acquired by larger companies. I had also been watching the hospital world. All of the hospitals in the Kansas City area were being acquired or were merging with other hospitals. These were all attempts to create efficiencies. Governmental funding was also being scrutinized, and attempts were being made to find more efficacious ways to provide services. We had just seen significant reform efforts in both the medical and mental health fields. Due to these discussions, the members of this think tank were in agreement that we were about three to five years away from the start of managed care or privatization in child welfare.

---

## "The only thing worse than being blind is having sight but no vision."

— Helen Keller —

---

I returned to Kansas and began talking with directors of various children's organizations. The response I received was rather dumbfounding and reminded me of this Helen Keller quote: "The only thing worse than being blind is having sight but no vision." Most believed that no such transition could occur in this field. Others had no idea what managed care or privatization was, but I could feel the trepidation among them. What I found was that providers, although in agreement that system change was needed, were comfortable with the status quo of keeping their beds filled.

I knew change was coming to our world, but I didn't know when it would occur. I remember a mayor of Cleveland privatizing a city transportation system in the mid-1990s. The governor of Wisconsin, Tommy Thompson, privatized other state functions, but as yet no state had attempted to privatize an entire child welfare system. Then I read about an experiment in New York to try to work with some foster children placed in five child welfare organizations. These agencies were given the responsibility to reintegrate foster children safely home or to move them to adoption. As soon as I read about the experiment, I called the New York commissioner to ask if I might visit with him to learn more about their new initiative.

The visit was enthralling. While I was there, I met with the leading researcher who was tracking this experiment. He was from Chapin Hall at the University of Chicago. Over the next couple of decades, I served on a number of panels and state advisory groups with this researcher. What I knew was coming, and what David Liederman had tried to predict had in fact arrived in a segment of New York. No one, however, could have predicted that Kansas would be the first to attempt a statewide system reform in this field.

# 13

## Pioneering Child Welfare Reform

When Bill Graves was elected governor of Kansas in 1995, he inherited the class action lawsuit against the state for inadequate child welfare services that had originated in 1989. He also learned that the legislature, during each subsequent year, had debated about whether or not to add money to a system deemed too big and too cumbersome. There was considerable discussion about reducing the size of SRS. Many legislators felt the size was too great to adequately manage. As a result, the governor and the legislature created a new department, Juvenile Justice Administration, that in effect removed the juvenile offender programs from SRS. Thus, the 1990s were a decade of major social change in Kansas, and SRS was at the heart of the change. Most of the change was led by the governor, a powerful president of the Senate (Dick Bond), the secretary of SRS (Rochelle Chronister), and her new commissioner (Teresa Markowitz). The governor and his wife were in the process of adopting a beautiful baby girl, and he was determined to impact the lives of other children. By making the decision to privatize child welfare services, he improved the way Kansas child welfare services were delivered.

Ultimately, by doing what the governor did to change the entire child welfare system, Kansas was the first state to fulfill what David Liederman's brain trust had predicted. It was also the first state to successfully exit one of these class action lawsuit settlements. In fact, the lawsuit was terminated only four years after the governor privatized the child welfare services.

During 1995, we received an announcement from SRS saying they would be hosting a public meeting and wanted child welfare agencies to attend. Oftentimes, these unplanned meetings were to discuss some element of the state's budget or perhaps to share that there was a program or major staff change to be introduced. No one expected to hear that the state of Kansas was to become the first state to privatize its child welfare services.

We were informed that the governor had decided that services would be undergoing major, statewide change. This was to become part of the state's settlement agreement with the Children's Rights organization. The lawsuit concerned not only the case management function but also protective service investigations. The state was divided into five regions with regional family preservation and foster care requests for proposals (RFPs) as well as a statewide RFP for adoption. In foster care, the division of labor under the new contracts pertained to SRS maintaining the investigation phase. Contractors would become responsible for the case management functions following the SRS recommendation and the court's decision to adjudicate a child as in need of care.

The announcement was quick; however, the reaction to it was almost the opposite. Most of the non-profit organizations in the state (approximately 40) were almost frozen in time. The reactions ranged from total disbelief to doubting that this could happen to a fear response. From my view, fear was the prevailing reaction. Notably, the statewide social work association and schools of social work were very resistant to this change.

During the weeks following this announcement, I received numerous calls from for-profit companies wanting to join KVC in offering a combined bid. The plan suggested by these companies was that since we had never performed under a risk-based contract they would provide the administrative services while we would provide the direct services. For this, they would receive a percentage of the total contract, which would be paid to them first, leaving the remainder for service provision. In that it was our goal to help lead this pioneering effort, I believed it was important that we learn to make these important administrative decisions as well as direct as much funding as possible to services. I advised these groups that we would not be interested in partnering with them. We had received these calls because KVC, by this time in our history, was the largest organization in the state, and many felt we would be a most likely recipient. In addition to KVC, United Methodist Youthville (UMY), located in Newton, Kansas, was also sought out by at least one for-profit company to partner with. UMY initially chose to partner with the for-profit company.

Over the weeks that followed, the saying most frequently used by our leadership was, "The only thing scarier than getting a contract is not getting it." We understood from the beginning that massive change was coming, and we could either be impacted by the change or we could help drive it. We knew that actually being awarded a contract came with tremendous risk, but we were not deterred. While we were fearful, it was a healthy fear. It was not a fear of change but of the many unknowns. We believed we had the right values, culture, and drive to make a difference. We never second-guessed our decision, although the initial learning curve would prove to be immensely steep.

Among other things we had to learn was how to bid on a risk-based contract. To learn more about the bidding process, the state held a number of meetings for potential bidders to discuss current costs and the training that would be needed to legally fulfill the case management responsibilities.

Regarding the bidding preparation, the state officials identified the amounts they had been paying for the services for which they would now be contracting. However, a common phrase we began to hear at each of these meetings when we asked for the supportive detail was that there was no aggregate data available. We, of course, were interested in particulars, such as the current placements of all children in care and the cost of each type of care and other supportive services. What we routinely heard was "no aggregate data available."

This was not to imply in any way that the state leadership was not fully committed to this system change. They not only were in favor of the change but helped drive it, shared the pain of the initial setbacks, and never did anything but share responsibility for them. To say that Rochelle Chronister and Teresa Markowitz, secretary and commissioner of SRS respectively, were standup women would be like saying the Leaning Tower of Pisa had a slight tilt. They were fully committed to making this new system work for children and families. There was simply no database on children and families and their services at that time from which to derive this important information.

Of the approximately 40 non-profit organizations in the state, only about five actually bid on the initial contracts. Even without all of the information about costs of care, numbers in types of care and other important pieces of information, we bid on two regional family preservation and foster care contracts and joined as a primary subcontractor in a statewide adoption bid. While we believed that each of these services belonged with a single contractor in each region for the sake of continuity for children, families, the courts, and other stakeholders, the state believed that to be too much for any entity at the start.

# 14

## Great Challenges Yield Great Rewards

Successes are rarely permanent, and failures are never enduring. The best you can do is your best every day. Consistent high performance accumulated over time equates to real success.

Unfortunately, using the figures and information provided, we severely underbid the initial contracts and initially lost a lot of financial reserves. Fortunately, we were not alone in our underbidding of the contracts. Recognizing that there had been too little information to accurately bid these contracts, Secretary Chronister orchestrated a one-time financial correction, allowing the successful bidders to get their financial feet on the ground and create better cash flow. This was essential if this privatization experiment was to be successful.

There were many daunting early tasks necessary to develop the infrastructure to support these regional operations. Some of the most significant tasks included the creation of a transportation system for thousands of transports for visits, courts, and medical care; the creation of a database of all available information on children; the creation of a 24/7/365 crisis response system and admissions department; the development of a strong network of service providers; and the development of training for staff members, foster families, and providers on an entirely new system and model.

During the first month, we had 4,000 transports of children that had to be done both timely and safely. We also had to account for our case managers needing to learn their new roles. One problem we faced early was that our case managers were reluctant to recommend that youths on their caseloads be returned home. The case managers, not knowing yet how to assess for a safe reentry into a child's home, chose to leave children in care longer than was necessary. Their action, along with the new entries constantly coming into the system early on, created a backlog of children in the system. This was part of the learning process but nonetheless resulted in my needing to acquire another facility to house these children.

Another early problem pertained to the number of licensed staff needed. Providing the case management responsibility was a new function for us, and we needed to learn quickly. With responsibility for the Kansas City area, there were close to 2,000 foster children for whom we initially became responsible. We did not take this responsibility lightly and knew we still had much to learn regarding the case management functions. While it was initially believed that many experienced state employees would transition to the newly identified contractors, this did not occur. This meant that multiple contractors in each region across the state were desperate to hire licensed professionals, leading to an early hiring war that further complicated startup and financial operations.

In my lifetime, I have learned that nothing worth having comes easily. It has been through hard life lessons that my greatest learning has come about. This was to be another great learning example not only for me and the KVC team but for all of the other contractors and their staff members. We had much to learn about case management responsibilities, including managing the frequency of home visits, assessing home environments for safety issues, safely increasing urgency and timeliness to permanency, safely projecting reunification dates, learning about required documentation, and creating effective court reports to judges.

Another complicating factor in our learning the case management role was that it was often being taught to our staff by SRS employees who had been providing this service and were now monitoring our staff. Many of these state employees who had been providing case management felt they had been transferred to new jobs because they had not been doing good work. In reality, they had been doing the work in the way the old system operated and in the way they were trained. But this was to be a system change. The old system had been very crisis oriented and built around moving through levels of care. There was no urgency for permanency for a child and no drive to get them home or to adoption.

Having the state workers train contractor staff brings to my mind the old story of a young girl watching her mother bake a turkey. As the story goes, the mother cuts off one third of the bird, throws that part away, and then bakes the remainder. When the girl asks her mother why she does it that way, her mother says she doesn't know but that that's how her own mother always did it. Unsatisfied, the girl asks her grandmother and gets the same response. Finally, she asks her great-grandmother, who says she did it that way because her oven was too small for a whole turkey. So often people continue to do things over and over just because that's how it's always been done.

This system reform allowed the opportunity for change from the status quo. We trained our staff with our isms, and we followed them. The results were that more than nine out of every 10 children in foster care where we provide case management (Kansas) are placed with a foster family, and nearly five of those nine are placed with a relative or other family known to them. We believe in family-centered practice, and the child's parents drive the plan. And reducing fragmentation, everyone involved in a child's treatment plan is part of its establishment or at least is aware of the plan and responsible for fulfilling it, not just the case manager. In approaching foster care in this manner, children were able to move safely and more rapidly to permanency in their lives. But again, nothing worth having ever comes easily, and as was to be expected with an entire system-wide reform, there were many bumps in the proverbial road.

During the first four-year contract, most of those involved in the system reform were detractors. This generally occurred when it was realized that all parts of the system were included in this change. Judges were expected not to continue to use long-term foster care but to start ordering reintegration and adoption cases to be moved through the court system more timely. In other words, all components of the child welfare system needed to change. Again, it was as John Kennedy had said: "A rising tide lifts all boats."

---

## "A rising tide lifts all boats."

— John Kennedy —

---

As stated earlier, the statewide association of social workers and the schools of social work came out in opposition. In fact, one faculty member from one of the universities' schools of social work operated a group home for boys. The non-profit organizations that eventually won bids to provide case management services under the new privatized system would attempt to safely reduce residential services and long-term foster care, impacting this faculty member's business. While some other providers chose to change their business plans in order to reduce congregate care and include community-based services, this professor chose instead to close his group home as an act of resistance to this effort. He told me how angry he was that the young men residing in his group home would not be able to grow up in that home — despite the research that shows that children grow best in families and not in group homes.

Some faculty members also served on various citizen review boards, statewide task forces, and multi-disciplinary teams, and in the early reform transition, these members routinely complained that the social workers providing case management services were poor writers and did not have good social work skills. Contractor leadership found this almost humorous in that most of our newly hired employees were, in fact, graduates of those professors' programs. Detractors were sure, before even trying something new, that this new system was wrought with different problems. In reality, the foster care system had operated for many years with numerous identified gaps, as outlined in the ACLU's lawsuit. One such gap was the high percentage of children in some type of long-term congregate care setting, whether it was a group home, shelter, or residential care. Within 18 months from initial startup of the new system, residential-type services were dramatically reduced while maintaining the highest of safety standards.

Years later, most faculty members have not only accepted the transition to case management provided by private non-profit organizations but are working in a united fashion with them. Some are partners in multiple research grants that are displaying significant positive research findings. The system has only gotten better with proven outcomes, and the bar continues to be raised through research and collaboration with partners such as the area universities.

Perhaps it would be important to mention some of the early concerns and factors that further complicated early transition and added to the chaos. Once the state streamlined its responsibility to only the investigative portion, the state was able to address many more referrals and on a more-timely basis. This resulted in an increased number of referrals to us. At the other end, our new case managers were just learning to assess for risk before returning a child home. This was an extremely important lesson to be learned, and the case managers often erred on the side of safety by keeping children in care longer than was necessary. This slowed the number of children exiting foster care and returning home, which caused the numbers to swell.

Another unanticipated consequence was that the newly created Juvenile Justice Administration (JJA), intended to serve young juvenile offenders, had yet to create needed community services. Thus judges, ensuring that services would be provided to these youthful offenders, began adjudicating them as "children in need of care." With our "no-reject, no-eject" contracts, this guaranteed judges that the youthful offenders would receive services. While this met the judges' needs of accessing services, it further complicated our new role with the accumulation of many additional referrals. It also put further strain on placement resources, including foster families, and there was already significant confusion on the part of many foster families across the state.

Many foster parents were sponsored by the state prior to privatization. As a part of the reform efforts, the state-sponsored foster parents had to transfer to a community non-profit organization. There was tremendous confusion about roles and responsibilities. Change almost always provides opportunities for confusion, but it also provides an opportunity for dramatic improvement. However, during the process it's sometimes difficult to see the potential benefits.

Along with early confusion within the foster parent community, courts were reactive as well. Many judges were demanding a variety of actions to be taken, such as requiring that multiple staff members from both SRS and contractors be in attendance at every court hearing. As the CEO of the largest contract, I was asked to appear in multiple courts across the state. This was a very time-consuming but necessary part of the changing landscape. Once the decision was made to privatize the system, all hands were on deck with an array of requirements that had to be achieved. Unfortunately, only the contractors and SRS were initially actively involved in the change. Many other stakeholders felt caught by surprise.

There was little explanation or direct involvement of various audiences, including foster families and courts.

About midway through the first year, as confusion continued with little resolution, I approached our management team with an idea. I told them that I wanted to sponsor a conference for all of our foster families. I wanted families to enjoy a weekend getaway at a nice hotel where we could provide education and support but also thank the families for their services to children and families, as well as for their patience during all the changes. I believed that a conference would allow time for families to calmly ask the questions that needed to be answered publicly. So my thought was not only to invite our families to this conference but to invite several judges to come to serve on a judges' panel where they would offer the families an opportunity to better understand why some court actions were taken.

Getting the judges to serve on this panel initially did not prove to be easy. District court judges have plenty to do without adding to their workloads — especially a work assignment that occurred on a Saturday. While I was able to persuade some judges by phone, others I had to meet in their chambers to convince them why it was important that they take part. Somehow, I was able to get an initial panel in place. Something magical happens when judges discard their robes and meet with families and others who appear before them in their street clothes. Great learning can take place not only on the family side of the panel but on the judges' side as well.

Interestingly, now that many judges have participated in over 18 years of conferences, I have heard from several that they initially avoided me and my attempts to reach them because they did not want to participate. Yet, everyone later said that if I asked them again they would come. Once again, I had proven to myself that nothing worth happening comes easily.

As I remember it, my vision for the conference was not initially embraced with much enthusiasm by our staff. Remember, we were in the midst of a system reform and significant turmoil; staff were working very hard to keep their heads above water. And on top of that, I wanted this conference to be held during the December holidays — already one of the busiest times of the year in our field as staff continue with their regular job responsibilities and work hard to ensure that every child and family receives Christmas presents. But, as is tradition with our team members, it was not long before the infrastructure was set for this one-of-a-kind conference. It was held at the Overland Park Marriott, and as I recall we received a discount on all of the rooms. Our staff stepped up in a big way that year and every year since with continually growing assistance from many wonderful corporate sponsors, donors, and volunteers. Looking back on this early conference, our staff had to take a leap of faith with me to pull off this near miracle.

I wanted families to have free hotel rooms, free food, fun family activities on Friday night, and supervised outings for their children all day Saturday in hopes that this would be the enticement for them to want to participate. I also knew I had to tie the conference to training, and so while their children enjoyed activities all day Saturday, we could guarantee many of the families' required annual training hours. I wanted them to attend on their own volition, so it was necessary for each family to call and register.

Lastly, I wanted to offer not only to our parents but to our older children the opportunity to hear from a keynote speaker of merit who had a strong, positive message about foster care. I wanted the speaker to speak from experience, encouraging families to go the extra mile and to not give up on youths who may be testing and challenging them by acting out behaviorally. One of our isms was *Our first placement is also our last placement*, and we worked hard to minimize placement moves and the trauma that comes with the moves. I also wanted someone who would have a motivational message for our adolescent population.

---

♥ KVC-ism

## *Our first placement is also our last placement.*

---

Over the 18 years of this conference, that latter message became a primary focus. So KVC leaders like Renny Arensberg and I would search for great speakers who were notable or famous in their fields of acting, education, law, politics, etc. The one caveat I insisted on was that they had to have been a foster youth as a child, overcome their traumatic start in life, and gone on to achieve success. And they had to have an uplifting message. I literally interviewed each potential speaker before one was contracted to be our presenter.

This combination of education and motivation brought hundreds and hundreds of families each year to our conference. The speakers became better each year, and the word spread rapidly among our target audiences. I attended and opened every conference with the exception of one. Just as we were opening our second conference, I was given a note that my mother was very ill. I left the conference to be by her side. Sadly, she passed away shortly thereafter.

Now we often speak of our families as resource families because we know these families often do far more than just open their homes to deserving children. Many of these families adopt children. Other families help train new foster families, and still others mentor foster and birth families. So in our 2015 Resource Family Conference, we had about 2,000 participants take part in a simulcast of our keynote speaker across multiple states where KVC now provides foster care. Beyond the shared opening and the keynote presentation, the KVC organizations in the different states provided individualized training geared toward their respective state's needs.

This conference not only helped stabilize our family resources during that first tumultuous year but since that time has helped drive our mission and vision further by providing a wonderful venue. It has also served as a forum to share great research advances in trauma and brain science as well many other training initiatives such as depression and suicide prevention awareness. These wonderful and meaningful conferences could not be realized without the many dedicated staff and volunteers from around the country.

Another development that occurred during that first year had to do with our acquisition of a residential facility in the southeast part of the state. We added this resource to strengthen our service provision throughout the contract region, thereby strengthening our contract bid. In years prior I had only known of this organization as another provider in our association and knew nothing of how it was viewed by its community. Subsequently, I found out just how poorly this organization was viewed.

During the first year of Kansas privatization, I was involved in about 50 public meetings. One that I very much disliked was the one I held to respond to community concerns about the quality of services of the organization that we acquired. During that meeting, there were probably 100 neighbors and business representatives in attendance. After documenting the concerns expressed, I asked the audience to return in exactly one year to review our progress. In the meantime, I found new seats on the bus for a few key employees and sent Jackie Suttington and Jason Hooper to the newly acquired facility in Southeast Kansas to not only run it but to instill the KVC culture and model. I told them to fire all of their employees, if necessary, and start with new employees and new training. They did a great job. Within about three or four months, we had replaced nearly the entire workforce and trained a new one. In keeping with my promise, one year later I notified every person who had attended the first meeting to come to a second public hearing and tell me how we were doing. Not one person showed up for the meeting. Our improvement plan had been necessary and successful, but the resources and actions it took to turn this around were very distracting as we were also launching our new state system-wide reform.

Again, there were many challenges during the initial transition, but Kansas state leadership was determined to stay the course and improve services for children and families despite the opposition. It's rarely a good thing when the governor calls you in your office at 7:30 in the evening but that's what Governor Graves did. He called to ask if there was anything he could do to help me in this period of transition. While I appreciated his candor, the system had to work through the pain of startup. Years later, when I was meeting weekly with the Nebraska governor and as KVC was working through system change in that state, I would often reflect on Governor Bill Graves' call to me that one evening. I have, in fact, met on multiple occasions with governors in every state where we operate, either as a provider or a major contractor, and met with the minister of social and family development in the country of Singapore, but nothing has made such an indelible impression on me as that call from Governor Graves.

The start-up phase had clearly been challenging. In fact, every system change I have witnessed has initially been challenging. What some began to forget was what the system looked like before system change was introduced. During the Kansas privatization process, when all parts of the system were being asked to change following the class-action lawsuit, many began to glorify the old system. This is truly an interesting phenomenon that I have seen occur in system reform in various states: the old system begins to look better as changes occur. It may not be right, but it is a reality of system reform.

These were challenging times not only for KVC but for the other contractors as well. Each contractor had, in fact, stayed the course and had helped change the system. By the end of the first four-year contract, many achievements had been realized, as evidenced by the state successfully exiting the class-action lawsuit. Consistent family preservation, foster care, and adoption services existed across the state, safety rates were some of the highest in the nation, staff caseloads had been reduced, re-entries into foster care were dramatically reduced, crisis support was available 24/7/365, adoptions had significantly increased, and more siblings were kept together and closer to home. In subsequent audits, Kansas finished toward the top when compared to all other states. In addition, the state set the bar for reducing children being referred to residential programs. In fact, at KVC we closed about 100 residential beds within our first five years as a contractor.

These initial contracts were to be in force for four years. As it happened, in the third year of the contract, preparation began for the next round of bidding. The bidding process was substantial. The finished bid documents were as thick as city phonebooks used to be before the digital age. They were massive, and I believe we reproduced about 12 copies for the evaluators. Anne Roberts and Sherry Love used to joke that we should put a sentence somewhere in the middle of the document that read, "The first person to read this sentence and call us will receive a $100 gift card." Of course, we never included such a sentence, but it was an exhaustive process not only for the writers of the document but for the readers as well. It took weeks or sometimes months to write and review.

By the end of the first four years, we led the state in all of the outcomes initially identified by SRS. What we knew, but was not widely understood, was that we had gone through the preponderance of the initial confusion, and things had already begun to stabilize. Yet, even with so many demonstrable gains, the initial turmoil of system change was not lost on the secretary of SRS. Gaining stability in the system appeared to be the driving force, and spreading out responsibility to other contractors, in my opinion, was what the secretary believed would help stabilize the system. In the next contract awards, KVC and United Methodist Youthville each maintained one region of foster care and each lost one region to new bidders. The third contractor, Kansas Children's Services League, had received one region initially and had subsequently retained that one contract. To the KVC staff, our loss of one region was taken very personally.

In the years to come, KVC continued to win expanded contracts in this public bid process (50 percent of the state of Kansas). As of this writing, we are the only remaining foster care contractor of the three originally selected. As a result of our outcome successes in Kansas, we were asked to assist in providing services, consultation, or training in numerous other states.

# 15

## Becoming Data Driven

Lewis Cass has said, "People may doubt what you say but will believe what you do." By 2016 we were tracking mammoth amounts of separate data entries as we annually touched 60,000 lives across multiple states and services. But in the beginning, having limited IT equipment and personnel, we were challenged to find our equilibrium in the technological world. Necessity, it is said, is the mother of invention. The software systems that have been invented by our own professionals and now fully integrated into our work are truly state-of-the-art systems. They were developed out of our necessity to successfully demonstrate achievement of outcomes as our service industry instituted accountable measures overnight. Ultimately, our social work staff fully embraced data; they never saw individual children or families as numbers or statistics, but used data as an additional tool to guide or provide evidence of good practice and effectiveness.

> **"People may doubt what you say but will believe what you do."**
>
> — Lewis Cass —

With the onset of privatization and risk-based contracts we had to make wise decisions to guarantee we were improving outcomes and, therefore, the quality of care in a financially sound manner, and we had to make them fast. In order to do so, we needed to have reliable data, which was highly unusual in the field of child welfare at the time. It was during this period that observers would hear comments like, "Social work is more of an art than a science." I wholeheartedly disagreed with this assessment. This "art" or subjectivity was one of the primary reasons that children and adolescents were maintained in foster care for years in some cases. While the state had "no aggregate data available" on children and families, this reform created the opportunity and, for us, the necessity to apply both science and data to this field.

A lot of major changes occurred during my tenure, but none was more important than the implementation of our computerized data system. While we began collecting some data in the 1980s, it was not until privatization that we began collecting data in earnest to make better decisions. This was not only a good idea; it was a must if we were to remain solvent while delivering services in risk-based contracts.

I remember how Bruce Linhos, CEO of the Children's Alliance, and I had tried three or four years earlier to convince SRS officials to buy a fairly simplistic tracking system being demonstrated by a private company in Des Moines. As contractors, we could have been the beneficiaries of that early wisdom, but we failed to persuade them. In hindsight, by not having it, we were forced to develop our own and do it quickly, which was much better in the long run. We did search the nation to see if there were any software programs we thought would truly help us but found nothing. It's important to remember that Kansas was the first state to relinquish its foster care operations to a non-profit organization. Therefore, there were no readymade road maps for us to follow. And no state had developed the kind of data system we needed in order to be successful, so we had to develop one.

We began developing software programs to help us keep track of the anticipated 2,000-plus children to be referred to us during the start of privatization. The contract required that we accept physical custody of each child referred to us within four hours of their notice. This large number of referrals was to occur over a number of days — I believe 90 — and not over multiple months or a year. Following transition, we knew that new children were being referred daily, while others were being safely discharged to their families or to an adoptive family. We had to know each day where all children were physically and where they stood in their course of care. Literally, this involved thousands of youths annually. At the time, we occasionally heard about different states where state officials had actually lost foster children. We did not want that to happen, and we knew we needed software programs built to help us track the large numbers of children whose safety, treatment, and reintegration were in our hands.

To put this situation into perspective, the month prior to KVC beginning as a pioneering privatization contractor in Kansas, we did not have a transportation department. The first month after all of the children had been transferred, we had 4,000 transports. This included new children coming into the system, children who for one reason or another moved to a new placement, and the more typical doctor, dentist, therapist, visitation, and court appointments where a family member or case manager was not available to transport. I believe this as much as any other factor best described the pressure we were under. So for us, we knew we needed information collected and put into a usable format so that we could not only track each child but evaluate appropriate progress for each child and family we served across a variety of domains in which we were being evaluated. To fully understand the complexity of this issue, you need to know that we initially served well over a third of all children and worked with 15 judicial districts, in each of which some children were reunified with their families daily as new children were referred daily to KVC. We reimbursed foster families and residential providers for each day of care per child whether they were there one day or 30 days. It was also important that we provided the foster families with financial resources to help them offset the costs of the children placed with them.

Initially, we struggled to get our arms wrapped around numerous issues. We had concerns such as ensuring that children were transported to the right locations and getting the right payment methodology to pay our foster parents. Foster parents were pleased that we had increased their per diem rates, which had remained the same for many years under the state system. We also reimbursed them more because we needed them to be part of our treatment teams since they spent considerably more time with the children than any of the professionals involved. It was challenging in getting the amount owed to each family. At the time, we were using paper forms that had to be completed manually before being submitted to our accounting department. This process needed to be done by a certain day each month so that our staff could verify and process the amounts on a timely basis to ensure prompt payment. This was a terrific problem.

As we began to build our system, it was not long before we began to notice Katie Easley, who was destined to help lead this initiative. Katie and her husband, Brett, were foster and adoptive parents, and they worked in direct service positions at KVC. But they also understood computer technology and data systems and could translate between these two complex worlds. Katie and Brent were key figures in bridging the translation of the two languages.

As our system developed, the bar was raised in decision-making and accountability throughout, from daily status reports on every child and contract outcome to treatment planning and court reporting. Also, we eventually set measurable outcomes for all of our departments for total accountability. Regarding payments, for example, we set an outcome that 97 percent of all monthly foster parent payments had to be error free. We monitored this target and continually identified barriers and created solutions. By doing this, we ultimately hit our mark and sustained that percentage or higher. However, it truly became a non-issue once we were sophisticated enough that staff and families could complete forms and send them electronically.

We have developed almost all of our software system ourselves. It is truly tailor-made to fit our individual program and contract outcomes in multiple states. But this is a system that continually grows and changes based on client and staff member needs. Suffice to say that if I were to attempt to list all of the components, it would take a book of its own. Notably, I will only work around the edges to give some additional highlights. For example, wanting to follow another one of our isms, *Our first placement is also our last placement*, we say that we want to match each new foster child with a family or a relative. We wanted to stop foster children from being moved to multiple placements. So our software development team, led by Lonnie Johnson, worked to create our Family Matching System, which allows admissions staff, who work around the clock 365 days a year, to consider numerous descriptive pieces of information such as a placement's proximity to the child's home, any health issues, whether or not there are siblings, any psychiatric diagnoses, etc., before placing a child with a foster family. It is a very detailed process, but with the help of technology it may take an admissions worker only seconds to complete.

We had to create a personal file on every child entering foster care. The file would always contain all available vital health, mental health, and educational data, placement history, court documentation, etc. Client log information, including visitation with foster and birth families as well as individual case planning meetings, had to be documented not only for the file but also for the courts, certain state personnel, and, in some instances, family attorneys. It was early in my history with KVC that I shared the vision for integrating child welfare with not only behavioral healthcare but with medical care. This was a truly unique approach in the field of child welfare.

We needed to both maintain and distribute documentation of any critical incidents (CIs), such as health emergencies, accidents, and suicide attempts. Critical incidents had to be charted for us to adequately understand our clients and to identify barriers. In addition, we began gathering hundreds of pieces of information on our clientele. As we did, we also began increasing our data collection on our inpatient psychiatric population. Again, Jason Hooper, the president of our hospital system, really drove this for our inpatient programs both before and after we later acquired an electronic medical record system.

Early on, some of us began reading about the Toyota process for building a car. I was intrigued when I read that any line worker could stop the production line if he felt something wasn't working right. Having a very successful engineer son-in-law who works for a competing car manufacturer, I knew two things: First, to stop the line would be an expensive process; and second, my son-in-law would not be pleased that I was modeling this after the Toyota plan (although I expect most companies had a similar plan). Nonetheless, this was very intriguing and exactly what we needed to empower our frontline employees. So we created a Magic System whereby any staff member who was using part of our database and either witnessed a problem or, even better, had an idea on how to improve it could submit a change order. Our information solutions staff would vet proposed changes with key personnel for unintended consequences. If there was a majority agreement about the change, the team would implement the change. Weekly, a notification of all changes was sent to all staff.

Our data system is very complex, and I could never do it sufficient justice by trying to explain it. I just know that our vice president of business information technology, Lonnie Johnson, and our talented team never rested in their efforts to create the system and to continuously improve it.

Today, we have a software data system any state would envy, and we are now looking at predictive analytics.

In this chapter I primarily focused on the early stages of the Kansas privatization and the evolution of our system. We have many rising stars in this growing department and in our other states who help write and implement the programs and continually develop innovations for our entire system. Jarrod Dungan in our Kentucky office is one of these stars. Jarrod is not a clinician but truly understands their functioning and with his computer knowledge has developed new applications for them. He has also helped integrate an existing system with a newer electronic health record.

# 16

## Improved Outcomes Through System Reform

When Kansas privatized its child welfare services, no state was using performance outcomes to determine how effective its services were. The Kansas SRS leadership was still referencing having no aggregate data. In 1996 and 1997, there were no federal guidelines such as the Child and Family Service Reviews (CFSRs). So, without having baseline data to compare from year to year, it was necessary for the Kansas leadership to create the first set of outcomes it desired to be achieved under the new reform.

There were some obvious considerations that state leadership used to develop the first set of reform system improvements. For example, it was obvious that their social workers were, in fact, overworked with caseload sizes reportedly reaching over 40 cases per worker. The recruitment of foster families was often given a lower priority due to the urgency and immediacy of investigations and out-of-home placements. Unfortunately, this lower priority of foster family recruitment often meant more children in congregate care settings and longer stays in state custody due to not having sufficient placement resources.

There were other problem areas as well. Family preservation services, for instance, were only provided in 44 of the state's 105 counties. SRS offices were open Monday through Friday from 8:00 a.m. to 5:00 p.m., which meant workers were only available during these days and times. Providers often either declined referred children or had them removed from homes, resulting in significant placement disruptions that often prolonged placement in the foster system. Approximately 75 percent of the children were placed with foster families, while far too many children remained in congregate care settings such as group homes.

And when children were reunified with their families, about a third ended up re-entering the foster care system, often due to a lack of necessary support to achieve stability. Legislative post audits continued to show that improvements were needed in the foster care system, which was predicated on the class action lawsuit filed against the state.

Once the system was privatized, there were numerous immediate system improvements. First, a 24/7/365 crisis system was initiated to support children, families, foster families, and providers. A 24/7/365 centralized admissions office was also created. Contractors were required to take physical custody of child referrals within four hours of referral on a "no-reject, no-eject" basis, putting an end to children remaining in inadequate settings such as state offices or hospitals waiting for a placement. Contactors worked hard to find appropriate placements for all foster children. Caseload sizes were significantly reduced. A full year of aftercare services was provided to families following reunification or adoption that, over the next three years or so, reduced the number of children re-entering the foster care system to as low as three to five percent, a significant improvement. Another important and immediate impact was a dramatic increase in the number of adoptions, which nearly doubled in the first year and has continually increased since that time. Probably the most profound outcome, especially given the early turmoil and confusion of system change, was that we maintained one of the highest safety rates in the nation for children in foster care. Following privatization, safety rates have never fallen below 99 percent.

# 17

## An Inpatient "Back Stop" and Community-Based Services

When child welfare system reform started in Kansas and children transitioned to our care, nearly a third of all children in out-of-home placements were living in a congregate care setting: a shelter, group home, treatment facility, or hospital. Only about 70 to 75 percent were living with a family. This was not uncommon and, in fact, is still true in some states. Within the first three years of privatization, KVC had safely reduced congregate care usage to single digits, no more than three to five percent in subsequent years. This is still possibly the lowest inpatient utilization in the nation. In addition, original average lengths of stay in our psychiatric residential programs have been safely reduced from 12 months to nine months to approximately two months today.

I believe we actually created some of the progressive national trends in child welfare by following some of our isms: *What would you want if this were your child?* and *Children grow best in families.* We would not want our own children sent to another state where we could not visit them and participate in treatment, and we would definitely not want them kept away from us for years in a state's custody. On occasions where we have accepted referrals from out of state into our residential treatment programs, we have done so to support a KVC subsidiary or service in another state. These were the result of all those in-state providers refusing to serve the children and the result of our interest in ensuring stabilization in the shortest period of time, followed by returning them to their home communities. While they are with us, we ensure contact and participation in treatment for their families by supporting travel and/or the use of technology tools for tele-therapy.

By staying true to these values, we focused on building community resources so families could better support children in their homes. While we'd always believed in this approach, privatization gave us the opportunity to put this practice into action. And the early realization that the contracts were significantly underfunded added increased urgency to "rightsizing" congregate care. We often spoke of being very appreciative for operating in a field where what is good for children and families is also good financially. Placing a child with a relative or with a foster family rather than in a group home, for example, is not only far less traumatic for a child but also far less expensive. Our professionals became experts at continually identifying gaps and barriers and working internally and with our network of providers to address them. In doing so, we were safely advancing a shift from more expensive and less effective residential services to family services and community support. In short, we were helping to shape the future of child welfare services.

Today, we are still consulting with states about how to reduce the number of foster youths being placed in residential centers. Some states believe that residential care is not needed in foster care, while others continue to over-utilize this service. We believe residential care is a necessary element of the treatment continuum. Clearly, youths do need inpatient hospitalization or residential treatment if they are intent on harming themselves or others. But this need represents only a small percentage of the population and only until stabilization has occurred, thus serving as a backstop. Then, treatment can be continued or completed in the community. This became the basis for most of KVC's future growth.

# 18

## Welcome to West Virginia

In 1999, about the time we were fully recovering from the early confusion of Kansas privatization and decisions were being made about the second round of contract awards, I had the opportunity to attend a conference on Cape Cod. It was advertised, among other things, to develop a psychological profile on CEOs. This is often a popular concept in that the better you know your profile the better able you will be at communicating with others who possess different personality styles. I responded, attended the conference, and to my dismay, my personality profile was used first. Being used first meant that my profile was projected on a large screen for everyone to observe and subsequently analyze. The person leading the exercise said my profile had been selected because I displayed more depression than any other attendee!

This may have been shocking to other attendees, but it was no surprise to me — nor to the presenter, as it turned out. Apparently, the presenter was well aware of the privatization efforts in Kansas. So, my depression scores were briefly explained as the outcome of the field of child welfare being turned upside down. That's exactly what was happening in Kansas during the statewide system reform initiative.

The fact that private non-profit organizations were given the opportunity to perform case management functions previously provided only by state governmental departments was being watched very closely throughout the country. These non-profit organizations had been asked to operate in risk-based contracts with prescribed performance outcomes, and resulting confusion among providers, court personnel, community providers, and foster families was making headlines. This grand experiment and pioneering effort had the entire child welfare community's attention. This attention was further heightened a little later when one Kansas contractor, a very old organization, went out of business because it could not pay its creditors.

So what I thought had been more of a Kansas concern turned out to be a well-known occurrence by most everyone attending the conference. The analyst referencing my profile concluded, among other things, that "Wayne would follow rules if they were his rules." I agreed with at least that part of my analysis. This was definitely a time of change and great confusion, and that comment reminded me that I needed to set the tone for many upcoming changes. Thus, I would follow my own rules.

My depressed personality had been described as understandable, but the second profile discussed perplexed all attendees. He was the CEO of an organization in West Virginia and had, at one time, been in a leadership position in the state's child welfare services. At present his organization was doing battle with West Virginia's Medicaid program and was losing badly. At the time of the conference, this organization owed Medicaid millions of dollars and had no apparent ability to repay the debt.

Following the conference, this individual asked to have a private meeting with me. At that meeting he said he had heard about the Kansas experiment with privatization and that he felt West Virginia was primed to consider something very similar. He then asked if I would be interested in acquiring his organization since I was very familiar with the privatization initiative and could help bring this experience to that state. I have always had a belief that you should never say never to an idea, and I was certainly not going to say no to expanding our impact by building services in other states. I had long thought about how that could happen.

I also believed that soon other states would (and should) follow the Kansas system reform. So I was not shocked by his suggestion that West Virginia might consider following our example. I also thought that if we were able to help with the transition in another state, this might be the best opportunity to position us for growth into other states so that we could apply lessons learned to positively impact more and more children and families.

By this time, I had already pursued opportunities in Missouri and had looked into services in Iowa and had actually been awarded a small time-limited foster care recruitment contract in Oklahoma. I told the executive that I might very well be interested. He indicated that he would return to West Virginia and discuss this with others and get back with me. Upon leaving that meeting, I had no idea if I would hear from him again, but I made note of his name and contact information, thinking I would follow up with him if I had not heard from him in a couple of weeks.

I found this man to be very engaging, but I could almost see bruises on his forehead from his figuratively bumping up against a much more powerful Medicaid bureaucracy. He had some good ideas, but he could never be successful approaching an entire state system in the manner he was using.

A few weeks later, I was sitting at my desk on a Monday morning when I was told by my assistant that a representative from the West Virginia attorney general's (AG's) office was holding on a phone line for me. More than a little curious, I took the call. After brief introductions, I was asked if KVC was interested in acquiring the West Virginia organization. We had already been vetted by Medicaid leadership regarding our good history of service provision. I replied, "Yes." I was then told I needed to come to West Virginia as soon as possible to view the organization, complete the due diligence, and then meet with the AG's team, which I later learned was composed of the commissioner from Medicaid, the secretary from the Department of Health and Human Resources, and their respective attorneys and deputies. The AG's office had already filed its intention to foreclose on the organization with the court, and a court date had been set.

So I quickly put together a team of attorneys and accountants, which included Tom Mullinix, who was a KVC board member and a lawyer knowledgeable in law and finance, and one of his associates. Our CFO, Paul Klayder, and our COO, Anne Roberts, were also included, and I rounded out the team. While the attorneys and accounting team began assessing the organization's books, Anne and I began meeting with state leadership, the organization's program staff, and other community stakeholders. The organization had numerous offices across a large area of the state. A review of the services and staff in several offices was conducted, as well as meetings with regional state offices. (Anyone not familiar with this beautiful state might be shocked to know that what appears to be a short distance on a map can require hours to reach due to winding, mountainous roads.) Of interest to me was the emphasis on community-based services, as opposed to inpatient care. As discussed earlier, a significant lesson learned in Kansas was that congregate care use could significantly be reduced when opportunities for community supports for children and families were increased. The services, predominantly in-home behavioral healthcare and foster family care, were in keeping with the KVC culture, isms, and vision.

We determined that we could make the organization financially viable if we closed specific offices and if the debt could be magically waived. Regarding the programming, the Medicaid commissioner told us he did not want to lose the valuable services to so many children and families but had lost confidence in the current management. The state was required to provide statewide coverage, and this organization was one of very few providing mental health services and the only one providing services in certain rural areas of the state. In addition, they were the only ones providing home-based mental health services at the time. Again, a lesson learned was the effectiveness of serving families in their home environments where change must occur as opposed to office visits.

The clouds of doubt were beginning to lift, yet the AG and the Medicaid staff members were adamant about certain points. One, the existing administrative staff had to be terminated as they'd lost confidence in them. There were also some practices that had to be eliminated. I agreed with the AG on all of those points. The elephant in the room, however, had not been addressed. There was still the matter of the debt to the state, which totaled millions of dollars in penalties.

After our team had determined that we could be of value, could make this successful, and could agree to the AG's conditions, I said we would move forward with a few caveats. First, there was no way we would assume the debt; that had to be agreed upon before going any further. We would be willing to assume their assets, which were mostly "blue sky," meaning there were few assets, agreement for continued referrals from the state, and limited goodwill. I indicated we would be willing to immediately hire their employees, less the administrator, which was a big bargaining chip for state officials who did not want a large number of staff members to be left unemployed and did not want a gap in services. Ultimately, other employees would be evaluated individually as to their effectiveness.

As part of our negotiations, I insisted that the Medicaid office increase its auditing of our newly acquired organization. Medicaid had been randomly appearing at this organization's offices around the state on a frequent basis, with the findings resulting in financial penalties. I was determined that they would continue to audit us on at least a monthly basis, although I wanted them to hold us harmless from any penalties for a minimum of six months. I also insisted that during this time they work closely with our financial and program staff in providing training until we clearly understood the Medicaid financial discrepancies and had a chance to make corrections to prevent what had led to such significant penalties and mistrust.

Their need to maintain the statewide services apparently outweighed the need to push for repayment of millions of dollars. Thus, they agreed to our conditions, and a judge later allowed us to acquire the organization by closing it down at midnight one day and reopening it under a new name the next morning. As I recall from being in court that day, certain creditors were upset, but others accepted their plight and signed new office and equipment leases with us so that services to children and families could continue uninterrupted.

Interestingly, just before I received the call from the West Virginia AG's office, we had received word from the state of Kansas that we would only be awarded one region of the state instead of the two we currently managed. In my opinion, the eventual and very painful loss of one of the Kansas regions made our West Virginia acquisition even more powerful. The loss was particularly troubling because KVC was then leading in all of the performance outcomes and had stabilized following what had been a tumultuous start to system reform. The safety rates, a performance outcome everyone reviewed, had actually never been higher. But by moving vigorously into West Virginia, we were able to keep most of our well-trained and highly motivated staff in the areas of corporate services and infrastructure. We were also able to offer direct care positions to any who chose to relocate.

Today, we have a high percentage of employees with 10 or more years of service to KVC, and there are many others with 15 years or more. It was repeated decisions like being willing to acquire another company that allowed us to create new positions for staff and keep high-performing staff members challenged and energized, including in such areas as IT and software development, human resources, development, and accounting. KVC was able to keep much of its talent, thus allowing the organization to continue to develop its infrastructure.

I had been contacted by the AG's office the week before Christmas, and by the end of December, we had basically acquired the organization. Technically, we had to wait until after the court date, but, in reality, the deed had been done. I truly believed that the services were important and that West Virginia's child welfare system was ready for reform because there were so many children remaining in care for years and the state was sending so many out of state. On one of my first trips to West Virginia, I read a lead story about the cost of child welfare. The story was about many youths being sent out of the state and the millions of dollars it was costing West Virginia. Besides being far from their families and home communities and their involvement in their care, these costs were reported at about $25 million and rose to about $40 million over the following 15 years.

But early in our entrance into the West Virginia system, I sincerely believed we could nudge the state leadership into considering system reform. My thought was to introduce their leadership to the Kansas initiative and, in particular, to discuss the KVC system and the proven outcomes achieved for children and families. At KVC, we had stopped the pattern of sending youths out of state for treatment purposes and had almost eliminated the utilization of group homes and shelters. At that time, only three percent of Kansas youths in foster care where KVC was providing case management services were in any congregate care setting, and those youths were in hospital or psychiatric residential treatment due to acuity and safety issues. Our safety rates were among the highest in the nation, exceeding 99 percent. I was a firm believer in change and thought that alone would cause them to want to model after our system.

My plan was simple. I had personally invited the secretary of the Department of Health and Human Resources (DHHR) to come and spend time with us at KVC. But in doing so, I offered to host not only the secretary but other members of his leadership team. He accepted the invitation and brought the commissioners of Medical Services and

Behavioral Health as well as a couple of deputy secretaries. I also agreed to host the current Kansas secretary and the corresponding Kansas officials. I thought by being as transparent as possible about the process that I could further this initiative. I felt strongly that by the time they left they would be convinced to privatize their system.

Surprisingly, within the following week after they returned to West Virginia, I received a call from the secretary saying that I had better get some positive messaging out. Apparently, the secretary and his team returned to Charleston to find a front-page article in the newspaper about the negative impact of privatizing the child welfare system. The leading residential providers in West Virginia had heard about the trip to KVC and were resisting any attempt to change their broken but, to the providers, known and financially viable system. They had gone to the newspaper and expressed their anxieties. If a story can be controversial, a newspaper will print it. This is the same newspaper that about every five years would write extremely negative articles about the child welfare system in West Virginia and how much it cost to maintain children in foster care placed out of the state. It always appeared to be an oxymoronic juxtaposition for the newspaper to take. However, the adage that newspapers will print stories based on the concept that "if it bleeds, it leads" rang true. There was such inconsistency in calling the state to task for not making system changes, then objecting to their efforts when state officials did try to change it. This phenomenon is not peculiar to West Virginia. I have heard officials in other states talk about wanting to engage in such reform but openly expressed an unwillingness to engage because of the usual pushback from internal groups affected by the change or from the media. People tend to support change as long as it doesn't affect them personally.

I, along with other KVC team members, did go to West Virginia to talk with members of the press, legislators, and the DHHR leadership at that time and in years since. This was only marginally successful until we met with representatives from the biggest residential providers. In fact, we invited representatives back to our corporate offices in Kansas. After that meeting, the tide began turning; however, by then the DHHR leadership had changed and a new secretary had been appointed. The new secretary and her team had less enthusiasm for system change. Another difficulty in driving change in child welfare is the turnover of states' leadership. The most recent average tenure I've read for states' top child welfare position is 18 months. This is truly one of the largest drawbacks to reform in many states. I give credit to many delegates and senators in West Virginia for their willingness and openness to change.

During this time, Anne Roberts came back from a child welfare/behavioral healthcare conference in Arizona. She said that one of the sessions she attended was on outpatient mental health therapy. In that session, the presenter made the comment that if you were a mental health provider in West Virginia, you might as well leave the state because they had the lowest reimbursement for this type of therapy in the nation. This was disheartening to us in that we knew a lot of money was being spent on out-of-state placements for foster children but without effective outcomes. We knew this was a very expensive option, and the returns on this approach had been deplorable. The status quo is always enormously challenging.

While attempts at system change are always hard, the learning for us was to consider the impact on existing providers and the judges/courts and not just the state leadership or the legislature. Years later, our governmental and legislative liaison in West Virginia was riding on a plane after returning from a business meeting and happened to be sitting next to the incumbent DHHR secretary. He mentioned to our liaison that his biggest mistake as secretary was not attempting to privatize their services. Inertia is always a major obstacle.

In January of 2013, as I was driving back to my office in Kansas with other KVC leadership following attendance at a meeting in Topeka,

I received a call from our governmental liaison in West Virginia. This is a call I will never forget. Our liaison started the dialog by asking me if I would be interested in acquiring a West Virginia naval base that was being decommissioned. Stunned, I started chuckling and replied, "A naval base?" He told me that he had just been contacted regarding the upcoming availability of a naval base in Sugar Grove, West Virginia. He added that it had been determined no armed services organization or state entity had interest, and therefore he had been asked if he knew of a non-profit corporation sophisticated enough to use it to create a community benefit. He informed the caller that KVC was the only organization he knew of that could do this, which resulted in this phone call.

Knowing the state was landlocked, I repeated, "West Virginia has a naval base?" His response was something like, "We actually have three." I remember laughing a bit more, and then he added something like, "Wayne, it was another 'Byrd Dropping.'" I had been in West Virginia long enough to know that meant a federally funded project brought to the state by the very powerful Senator Robert Byrd. Robert Byrd served in the Senate from 1959 until his death in 2010 and had been the Senate majority leader in the late 1980s. During this time, he championed many improvements and projects to benefit his home state.

Although I pride myself on never saying never, after a little more conversation I acknowledged that I didn't believe we had a good usage for the property, which included 120 acres and several beautifully maintained buildings. Even if it were just handed to us, it would have been expensive to maintain.

Perhaps two weeks passed before I heard from our liaison again. This time he asked me if I would have any greater interest if the property could be conveyed to KVC with an accompanying financial allocation that would support the maintenance and program startup costs. This time I became more intrigued and asked for a tour of the base. Unfortunately,

I was not available on the same date that the commander of the base was available. So I asked Anne Roberts and another staff member to tour the base. This was still a time in West Virginia when hundreds of children and adolescents were sent out of state for treatment purposes. Although our focus was on expansion of community-based services and not institutions, we had long before considered opening a "backstop" facility in West Virginia that would serve the many youths being sent out of state. Again, our belief was that if we could keep children closer to their homes, it would be easier to involve their families and successfully reunite them. We also knew that youths sent out of state remained there far longer than we would need to help stabilize them and transition them home. And, of course, funding for these services would impact the West Virginia economy as we created new jobs with accompanying health insurance. This was our thinking regarding a possible, sustainable service prior to visiting the facility.

Following a visit to the site and after seeing all the facilities, Anne called me and said that its location was really not conducive to increased family access and involvement for residential services, but that it was a perfect small college-like environment for our young adults. That assessment started our research into services for older youths who were aging out of foster care. What we found was that only two percent or so of youths who transitioned directly from foster care were successfully completing any post-secondary education. There was definitely a gap in services for this population. Empowered with this knowledge I, along with Anne and others, began meeting with community college executives and their financial officers, Health and Human Services professionals in Washington, DC, General Services Administration (GSA) professionals, and secretaries overseeing foster care programs in multiple states, as well as legislators and the governor in West Virginia. We developed a strong business plan for repurposing the naval facility into a specialized career college with a focus on young adults emerging from the foster care system. The resulting campus would combine innovative educational methods with practical, in-demand vocational skills training built on an infrastructure of specialized health services. Emphasis was to be on the creation of post-graduation, on-the-job training opportunities and career placement support. No such program existed then, nor does it yet today.

The next step was to take our research and proposed business plan to our board of directors. Today, I still hear comments from board members who were in attendance that evening. John Barnes, one of those board members, routinely talks about how shocked he was during that meeting. His perplexed response was, "Who does this? Who brings a proposal about acquiring a naval base?" John added that he will never miss another board meeting.

I conducted public hearings, and gratefully leadership from most of the surrounding communities supported our efforts. But what was originally presented as a fairly simple allocation of the property as a public benefit became a very cumbersome three-year process. Significant challenges and barriers continually arose, including renewed interest in the property from the state department in charge of penitentiaries. After about a year of delays, however, they withdrew their attempt to acquire the property due to the cost of necessary renovations, as well as very limited access to a workforce in the region.

Eventually, the GSA was given responsibility for disposal of the property and determined the best way was to put it up for public auction. Although no others had expressed interest during the three years prior, a number of entities became interested at this point, resulting in a bidding war. This was not something KVC wanted to be involved in. One of the bidders wanted to acquire the property and lease it back to us. The other bidder did not specify its intended usage. In the end, this last bidder submitted the winning bid but later reneged on it. At the time of this writing, the property is still sitting vacant and, unfortunately, will deteriorate over time unless a suitable owner becomes available.

In the meantime, KVC has continued to drive this innovative concept under the direction of Jason Hooper, who is considering alternative sites in the state. In fact, Jason Hooper and his team have been publicly acknowledged by West Virginia Governor Jim Justice for working to bring this specialized vocational college concept to West Virginia. It remains to be seen if this important program can be brought to fruition, but Jason and his team are working collaboratively with numerous potential partners to try to make this goal a reality. Many states recognize that youths in foster care cannot simply emancipate or age out at 18 and be expected to be successful with little to no support from caring adults. Certifying them in a vocation that would pay a livable wage, and transitioning them to self-sufficiency with a safety net in place is part of the answer. The other part of the answer lies in focusing on why only two percent are successful in existing post-secondary opportunities. Success requires more than just providing good course offerings. It requires providing support and encouragement to young people who likely have a history of trauma, failure, and rejection.

Today in West Virginia, KVC is a very highly respected and tenured organization — the largest foster care and home-based therapy provider — and a good partner to DHHR. We have many trusted staff members who have been with KVC for at least 10 years and some who were already with the organization when KVC acquired it. Our West Virginia leadership is very passionate and is working closely with DHHR to help usher in major changes in the state. In 2015, DHHR leadership started Safe at Home West Virginia, an initiative to return children who had been placed out of state back to their homes. KVC West Virginia is at the heart of this initiative and is actively supportive as one of the early contract recipients working to make this innovative approach become a reality. This initiative should be applauded and definitely encouraged. It will be far less expensive, and child welfare outcomes will improve. Of course, the true beneficiaries are the children who won't have to be banished from their families and friends for months or even years.

The obvious lesson learned is that change is almost always hard, and it will most definitely be resisted. Even a broken system begins to look good when compared to the necessary changes that all parties have to make in order for the system to operate differently or compared to the confusion that is sure to accompany any transition.

The state was paying much more for residential care than it was paying for in-home therapy, which helped to keep a child either in his own home or in an adoptive home if the child's home was deemed to be unsafe. While this practice has historically been the approach that West Virginia has used — maintaining as many as 400 or more children in residential care placements out of their state and hundreds more in similar services within the state — today this practice is changing.

# 19

## Piercing the Corporate Veil

It was sometime during 2007 that I received a call notifying me that KVC had been included in a research study funded by the Edna McConnell Clark Foundation. The study had been conducted by the Bridgespan Group, and their focus was to look at growth within all non-profit organizations in America whose primary service was to children and adolescents. I was told by the interviewers who contacted me from the Bridgespan Group that KVC was the third fastest growing non-profit organization — just behind a couple of organizations in New York — in the country. Interestingly, we also had substantial growth the year following their study. I then read in the national publication *Open Minds* that KVC was one of the most talked-about organizations in the country.

These occurrences prompted me to share this information at a following board meeting. I reported that growth had been the strongest in our contracting for the delivery of foster care services and in our expanding hospital program. I believe it was Scott Asner who, while discussing our significant growth in fields that encompass high-risk behaviors, questioned whether or not we had initiated adequate protection against potential litigation. That discussion resonated with all of us in attendance. While we had been able to discernibly allocate resources to our separate divisions, and correspondingly they were all growing substantially, clearly we were not as prepared as we should have been against potential lawsuits. As a result, we began looking at reorganizing our corporate infrastructure.

After some discussion and research, we began to consider a holding-company structure with separate subsidiaries. The intent was to keep a parent organization as the umbrella, providing consistent support services but no direct care services, ideally keeping it from being included in a potential lawsuit resulting from direct practice. It was also the intent that if there was litigation against any one subsidiary, it be contained in that one subsidiary so as to prevent the litigation from spilling over into any other subsidiary or the parent company. (The legal terminology for this initiative is called "piercing the corporate veil.") By creating separate 501(c)3 corporations for our hospital service and our services in different states, we were better able to contain risk. We also established a separate KVC Foundation at that time to serve as an entity for management of all KVC assets, as well as for additional fundraising to support all subsidiaries. Gratefully, KVC has had very few lawsuits throughout its history, and most of those were dismissed. Nonetheless, this was an essential element to help protect the corporation while driving safe mission-based growth.

A secondary benefit to restructuring into separate subsidiaries was that we could better identify and recognize our up-and-coming leaders. Transition to this new structure offered expanded opportunities to identify professionals beyond our presidents to include vice presidents, department directors, and other employees with specialized positions and to broaden roles and responsibilities. Obviously, well-deserved salary adjustments came accordingly as well. This allowed us to dig deeper into our employee bench depth and reward additional levels of leadership in the respective subsidiaries, as well as within our corporate infrastructure.

We began holding our management team meetings in different states where we had our subsidiaries. This allowed our management team opportunities to learn more about services and employees across all of our subsidiaries as each made periodic presentations to our team. This was a great way to continue witnessing individual talent while concomitantly receiving program updates.

# 20

## Becoming a Cornhusker

"People are always blaming their circumstances for what they are. I don't believe in circumstances," said George Bernard Shaw. "The people who get along in this world are the people who get up and look for the circumstances they want and, if they can't find them, they make them."

Over the years, I contracted with a number of national consultants who were aligned with our vision to keep me posted on child welfare and behavioral healthcare services and potential opportunities around the country. Gratefully, the contracts we have in other states came about through invitations from the respective states' leadership. However, I still kept in touch with these contacts and consultants in order to stay well informed about what was happening in our fields.

---

**"People are always blaming their circumstances for what they are. I don't believe in circumstances. The people who get along in this world are the people who get up and look for the circumstances they want and, if they can't find them, they make them."**

— George Bernard Shaw —

---

In 2008, following our submission of proposals for Kansas contracts and while waiting to learn whether or not we would be awarded any, I was contacted by one of these consultants. The lady was inquiring about my interest in a privatization opportunity in Nebraska. I told her that I was interested but needed more information. I subsequently called and made an appointment with child welfare administrators in Lincoln, Nebraska. (Conversation was permissible because no request for qualifications had yet been released.) The primary reasons given for this initiative included Nebraska ranking in the bottom five states on federal reviews and showing little progress on improvement plans, having more than twice the number of children in foster care per every thousand children than the national average, spending less per child than any surrounding state, and the potential of this new initiative to prevent federal penalties. Nebraska also had one of the highest uses of residential care in the country. The latter is understandable due to the history and reputation of Boys Town. I know the Boys Town leadership and the dedication of their staff; however, to be successful in this contract, residential usage had to be reduced. The goal often described in Nebraska was to "flip the pyramid" by moving the high numbers in out-of-home care to in-home services.

Anne Roberts and I explained the Kansas privatized system to their leadership and listened to their ideas as to what they planned to include in their eventual request for proposal (RFP). After listening to us, they apparently liked what they heard and added some of our thoughts into their RFP, including, as just one example, the importance of aftercare services. They, however, were not interested in giving the lead agencies case management responsibilities. Lead agencies would have no decision-making authority over entries into care, exits from care or placements, or services, yet they would have full financial risk driven by these key decisions. We explained that by not including case management responsibilities the service costs would very likely exceed the allocated funding. We suggested that separating those who could authorize the services for each family from those responsible to pay for services was a problem waiting to happen. One entity being accountable to both was what we'd found to be a key to success.

In Nebraska, this was to be a service coordination contract, providing a global or all-in budget, representing all funds identified as having been spent solely on services during the prior year, to the successful regional bidders. It was stated that there would be a case rate developed after one year when there was a greater understanding of actual costs. Ultimately, KVC was awarded the largest contract of all respondents, with responsibilities in the Omaha and Lincoln areas.

As we later found out, the author of the privatization movement in Nebraska was the former commissioner, who, immediately before the contracts were announced, resigned from his position to accept a different position in another state. This information, however, was not shared until after the contracts were awarded. About a year into this contract, I was told by the new administration that they were not and had never been in favor of privatizing Nebraska services. One of the many lessons learned in Kansas was that state leadership needed to be totally committed to the reform effort. A lack of commitment would fuel the detractors and likely derail the initiative. So, while this was disheartening, in every major change I have been involved with or have personally witnessed, there are always more detractors than proponents. Change is frequently wanted and usually very warranted, but when others realize their part of the service world must also change, frustration appears universal.

We began searching for the right person to head our Nebraska operations. As we developed a short list of names, one name kept emerging: Sandra Gasca-Gonzalez. Sandra had experience in Kansas working with state leadership, legislators, and contractors. Sherry Love, Anne Roberts, and I began a full-court press to hire Sandra, as we knew her from our Kansas contractor experience and had been impressed. I suspect that if Sandra had been a professional baseball player, she would have been like Babe Ruth who said, "Never let the fear of striking out get in your way."

Of course, most people remember the Babe for hitting 60 home runs in one year. Fewer people know that in the same year he set another record for the most strikeouts. Sandra was similar in that when something important was needed for children or families, her motto was to run with scissors. She was very passionate, competitive, talented, and therefore very respected in the field. She was also extremely competent and assembled a magnificent team that has continued to receive accolades for services rendered.

---

## "Never let the fear of striking out get in your way."

— Babe Ruth —

---

As contract recipients, we knew we must reduce the number of youths already in out-of-home care, especially those in residential care and in programs in other states. We began providing more home-based services and also stressed that community services be attempted before children were removed from their respective homes and placed in foster care.
To accomplish our initiatives, we sought out the regional mental health entities to increase services to this population. We also began urging the state to file for a federal waiver to allow for more funds to be transferred from foster care services to prevention services to help prevent foster care adjudication and children being removed from their homes unnecessarily.

This was a good plan, and the longer we were in the role of contractor, the more converts we made. But it is always hard to modify an entire system. Literally all entities affiliated with the child welfare system are affected. The list is long, but the primary entities were the judges and court workers, attorneys, state employees, providers, foster parents, and contractor staff.

One important part of our evolutionary journey occurred during the first year of this contract, when we began seeing some of the Nebraska organizations that had also won bids start to exit the contracts literally from the second month of service. This was astonishing to me and further complicated the reform effort. They closed or ended their services before the end of the first year. One of these organizations had over 100 sponsored foster families. Sandra heard a rumor that one of these lead agencies was taking bankruptcy and would be closing its doors on Friday of that week. So, she and I met with the owners of this for-profit entity to look at acquiring the organization. Unfortunately, the asking price was too high, so we walked away. We had great interest in transferring sponsorship of their foster families, as they were desperately needed, to help care for the large number of children in foster care. Remember, Nebraska at this time was removing children at the second highest rate per capita in the entire country, and we wanted to prevent the children from going into congregate care settings.

As one might expect, the foster families were by then very upset, not knowing what would happen to them and to the children placed in their homes. The families were free to align with any sponsoring organization but would not be compensated for the children in their care until they were once again sponsored by an organization. So a plan was rapidly made to hire the staff member who was in charge of the agency's foster family program and, in addition, offer employment to their case workers who worked directly supporting their foster families. We asked the caseworkers to call the families they worked with to let them know that KVC was very interested in becoming their sponsoring organization as early as that Friday evening so no reimbursements would be lost to them. The caseworkers were also informed that our staff would be available to them from Friday night until Sunday night of that same week. Then a number of our human resources and clinical staff drove from Kansas City to join Sandra and her team in officially hiring the staff, enrolling them in our benefit package, and completing the sponsoring process for the families.

By Monday morning, all of their families had joined KVC, and there was no lapse in services to children, payment to families, or salaries to employees. These swift actions were very much appreciated by these families and by our team, probably much more than by competing organizations who had also hoped to recruit a few of these families over time. Understanding that children and families can't wait, we knew the urgency and ensured the children would not go without care and families would not go a day without compensation. As of this writing, we continue to sponsor more foster families than any other organization in Nebraska and are continually recruiting more.

Despite significant efforts by many, this initial lead agency concept did not long endure. The global funds identified as available to support this initiative were significantly reduced prior to contract initiation. In KVC's regions, 3,042 children were identified as our responsibility at any given time under this contract, as per the prior year. In reality, that number ballooned to 4,700 within the first year and a half with the same funding. The global budget concept put lead agencies at great financial risk, as the numbers in care significantly rose with no corresponding increase in funding. It would have required adding significant funding. Ultimately, all but one of the original contractors made the decision to exit these contracts. One entity remained in the Omaha area as a pilot program. There was simply not enough money in the system to achieve the desired services, especially with the ratios of staff to clients that were required and the very high usage of residential services, which was very costly and slowed down achievement of permanency.

While KVC could not continue as a lead agency under this model, this important initiative established the foundation for our significant work in Nebraska today. One of Sandra's protégés, Jodie Austin, is president of KVC in Nebraska, and Jodie and her team have coined the ism *We don't sleep until you do.* This is a reference to how dedicated Jodie and her amazing team are as they work with both state employees and with the remaining lead agency staff to ensure support to every child and foster family. Jodie is truly a rising star in the KVC world, not only in Nebraska but in providing leadership and training throughout the country. One of her first training initiatives was with the Children and Family Services Administration (CFSA) in Washington, DC. Sandra Gasca-Gonzalez was, at that time, serving as its deputy secretary as a loaned executive from KVC. This was all after CFSA Secretary Brenda Donald visited KVC's programs in Kansas with several of her administrators and asked that we assist her in implementing the KVC model.

---

♥ KVC-ism

## *We don't sleep until you do.*

---

Today, we are the largest sponsor of licensed foster homes in Nebraska and serve hundreds of foster youths each day, as well as providing intensive family preservation and serving youths in the juvenile justice system.

Another great accomplishment our Nebraska staff attained was a very low disruption rate. Historically, children are moved from one foster home to another as disruptions in placement occur. Youths rarely disrupt from KVC families due to the training that families are given, as well as the individualized support by our staff. The children in our foster families traditionally remain stable. As of this writing, the stability rate is approximately 97 percent. Our Nebraska staff has also gained recognition for in-home family services.

In any new initiative, there are many lessons learned. The Nebraska contract proved to be no exception. For a while we had meetings every other week with the governor. We even had one Friday-night meeting in his home. In attendance with me were Anne Roberts, Paul Klayder, Sandra Gasca-Gonzalez, and Sherry Love. I also had more private meetings with the governor and his secretary of DHHS. In one of our regular meetings, after I made a comment about an assumption, the governor told me I should never assume. He said, "Wayne, you know what happens when you assume, don't you?" Then he proceeded to tell me. Yet, it was not five minutes later when he said to me, "I assume you will agree," and then he made a point. Without hesitating, Anne Roberts said, "Governor, you just told us we were not wise to ever assume." I may have laughed a little too loud at that comment!

Every state in the country provides child welfare services. In each state, one can find similarities with other states, but there will be some uniqueness. Nebraska was no different in that regard. There are points I agreed with and some I believed to be less desirable. I found their legislature to be more challenging simply because it is unicameral, meaning there's only one house of government. If you are elected to the legislature in Nebraska, you will be a state senator. It may be easier in some cases to get new legislation written, but it can also be harder to change a system of care. In most legislatures, there are two houses of government. The House, for example, may act as a check and balance to actions taken in the Senate. If you only have one chamber of government, it can be an easier or harder form of government, depending on your own viewpoint. To me, it was harder. But, Nebraska continues with its reform efforts, and we are happy to assist in that effort. Again, our Nebraska staff is working hard to find opportunities for children in foster care, and now in juvenile justice, to be placed with a foster family or with relatives rather than in congregate care. I am extremely proud of the work being done in Nebraska and of the very talented staff we have in that state.

# 21

## KVC Kentucky Pony

Over the years we have had a number of state officials, legislators, foundation representatives, and board members from states across the country who have visited our Kansas operations to learn about our networked programs. KVC Kansas is unique nationally in that our core services are extensive, are contained in one system, and include case management, which is different from the often-fragmented services provided in other states.

For example, children in foster care who are experiencing emotional pain and are in need of psychiatric hospitalization might be referred to a variety of hospitals or outpatient providers without any linkages or specialized knowledge of the intricacies of child welfare. In Kansas, our hospitals and all our outpatient therapists and case managers are trained in the same researched methodology. In states where we do not provide inpatient psychiatric care, we provide community-based services that help safely limit hospital usage, and we provide follow-up with our staff members once the patient or client has left the hospital. Our goal is a seamless delivery system that is not fragmented so that children don't linger in state custody as a result if they are in a foster care system.

It was in this fashion that we had a call from a consultant, Chris Groeber, who was working with the commissioner in Kentucky. I believe this was in 2009. After working through some logistics, a meeting was set for the commissioner of the Cabinet for Health and Family Services to visit KVC in Kansas. The commissioner accompanied the consultant to learn about our networked system. At the time, Kentucky's in-state residential services were being overused, and a couple of hundred foster youths were placed out of state in treatment centers.

During the commissioner's visit, we demonstrated that our complete system included how we used our "no-reject, no-eject" inpatient hospital and treatment center as a backstop, which prevented the practice of sending foster children out of state for treatment purposes. We further demonstrated how our case managers worked in conjunction with our inpatient programming and community-based therapists. Because the commissioner was sufficiently impressed, she invited us to visit Kentucky and to consider expanding our services to support children and families in her state. On one of my earliest trips to Kentucky, I was told that any visitor staying at least three days would be given a pony! While this was funny, I found quickly that Kentuckians take great pride in their horses and horseracing, and justifiably so.

Chris Groeber, who organized this visit for the commissioner, proved to be a valuable resource. A social worker with several years' experience, he was a trusted ally of the commissioner and was very knowledgeable about how the system worked in Kentucky. He was also very knowledgeable about what didn't work. He had done consulting outside of Kentucky and knew there were areas where the Kentucky system could be improved.

One of the greatest things Chris did for us was to introduce us to Liz Croney. Liz and her husband, Dr. Jim Clark, were co-owners of Croney and Clark, a private company providing behavioral healthcare services primarily in Lexington. I would describe this company as a very professional, boutique-type behavioral healthcare provider that was well respected by the local community and area courts.

Croney and Clark did not provide the usual services found in child welfare. The company's focus was on working with families by providing services in their homes, which we knew was most effective. We found our values and culture to be well aligned; this was a perfect match for KVC and for Croney and Clark. In fact, Liz Croney and I seemed to be on the same page when it came to the shared beliefs that (1) the priority should always be on the true needs of the children and families, and (2) it was possible to build a great organization by having a dual focus on values and performance. KVC could continue to expand its reach and lessons learned, and Croney and Clark could grow and expand services beyond what it was able to support as an independent owner. While Liz Croney was the primary operator of the company, Jim was at the time associate dean for research at the University of Kentucky's School of Social Work and was an excellent social worker, trainer, and consultant. Over the years we have asked Jim to assist us with various projects, and he is always there for us in providing the highest of quality consultation. We subsequently offered to purchase Croney and Clark and ultimately acquired the company. This was truly a great find for KVC. Croney and Clark has a multitude of wonderfully dedicated and very talented staff members who continue to raise the treatment bar for children and families in Kentucky.

Early on in our Kentucky programming, we agreed with the commissioner that the state needed a hospital and residential backstop that included a "no-reject, no-eject" admissions philosophy like we had in Kansas. This was one way to stop the flow of children to out-of-state facilities. We were encouraged not only by the commissioner but also by the lieutenant governor to pursue the development of a residential backstop. The lieutenant governor, a physician from eastern Kentucky, was interested in helping youths from his region of the state to receive treatment closer to their homes by having a facility built in the city referred to as the "Gateway to the Appalachians." We also received the support of the governor, who actually encouraged new legislation to be written in order to assist us in our effort to build this facility. Unfortunately, in the end we were stymied by the hospital association in Kentucky because it was not interested in having new hospital beds opened in the state without going through a significantly long Certificate of Need process.

Of course, we would only have been competing against hospitals with psychiatric beds and the for-profit, free-standing psychiatric hospitals. But the association was determined. I remember one day in the legislature when about 15 lobbyists were wearing large buttons with the words "Vote No!" in reference to our newly introduced legislation. We ended up going through a legal certificate of need process that was costly and not at all rewarding. But in the hearings, both Dr. Jim Clark and Jason Hooper offered strong rationale as they were put through a legal contestation that we were destined to lose.

But under the leadership of Liz Croney and her very dynamic team, our Kentucky services area and continuum has continued to grow. In fact, within the first three years, it was four times larger than when we acquired it. Much of this increase came from expanding the Diversion and Family Preservation Services after being awarded eight out of 10 possible statewide contracts (which deviated from the usual process of making these awards to several contractors). After these contracts had been awarded, many potential contractors that were not awarded contracts filed complaints with the Finance Cabinet; however, all of the complaints were summarily dismissed as groundless after a brief investigation. The push-back in Kentucky was, in fact, very similar to what I had witnessed in Kansas several years before. Most recently, with the rise in opioid usage and the rise in heroin abuse, our KVC Kentucky program received the largest grant award in the state to help combat this horrific epidemic. This $2 million grant allowed KVC Kentucky to expand this area of expertise significantly.

KVC's creativity has not ended there. This team, in partnership with leaders from KVC West Virginia, also helped the entire KVC network receive funding from the Department of Agriculture that enabled us to provide iPads for all of our foster parents nationwide. These iPads allow for better communication with foster children and families, including emergency therapeutic sessions. Many of the areas we serve are in very rural communities, and with inclement weather it becomes very challenging to reach foster and birth-family homes. And, to a lesser extent, educational enrichment opportunities are provided for children in foster care, who frequently lag behind, to get them to where they should be academically based on their ages. This team is truly making a difference for Kentucky children and families.

# 22

## Show Me State

In December of 2015, I learned of a potential opportunity with
a Missouri-based organization, the Niles Home for Children. This
organization has a long history in Missouri — over a century of service,
in fact. However, in 2015, it was experiencing extensive program and
financial setbacks. At that time, I was nearing my retirement date, so
before approaching this organization, I discussed it with our incoming
CEO, Jason Hooper. As a result, I called and made an appointment
with the organization's president, Rita Holmes-Bobo. The meeting was
fruitful, and so I arranged for Ms. Holmes-Bobo to tour our Prairie
Ridge Hospital and to meet with our hospital leadership and our
KVC child welfare leadership. We also wanted her to learn more about
Kansas services and to tour our corporate offices in Olathe. Clearly,
the purpose of these meetings was to introduce our depth and range of
services, as well as to introduce her to our various subsidiary and corporate leadership.

KVC was already serving many children from Missouri in our hospital.
I shared our interest in having the Niles Home for Children join the
KVC network as a subsidiary organization so that we could expand
our mission to impact even more children and families in Missouri. As
a result, I had the opportunity to meet on several occasions with Ms.
Holmes-Bobo and Niles board members to express and further discuss

our interests. In years past, I routinely called upon our chaplain, Reverend Dr. Jackie Suttington, to assist me in special-duty assignments. I had her join me in many of these meetings because she already knew individuals affiliated with Niles.

Eventually, I and two other competing organizations were invited to present our interests to the Niles Board of Directors. I was the final presenter of the evening. KVC was subsequently chosen as the organization with whom Niles would partner. Once this decision was made, I withdrew from further involvement and passed the baton to Jason Hooper. He and his team have since coordinated all the work necessary to make this a reality, including our development staff working with Ms. Holmes-Bobo toward necessary reconstruction of some of their outdated facilities.

I have no doubt that Niles, with its history of support in Missouri, and the added support of KVC, with its vision of creating a broader continuum of care, will help raise the service bar for children and families in that state as well.

# 23

## Going to Singapore

For nearly a decade, KVC has been affiliated with Glenn Saxe, MD, and his work with children who have experienced trauma. We not only bonded with Dr. Saxe and his team at New York University (NYU), but we helped drive his Trauma Systems Therapy methodology into different states and the District of Columbia. Our primary trainer was Kelly McCauley, and often she would be paired with Adam Brown, PsyD, a colleague of Dr. Saxe from NYU. Both Kelly and James Roberson, another KVC employee, created significant derivations such that we were able to develop manuals and other teaching materials to aid in the educational process for foster families, inpatient staff, and residential providers.

In addition to providing training to our staff, state employees, and public school employees in different states, Kelly and Dr. Brown presented at a National Child Traumatic Stress Network meeting held at UCLA. Among the attendees was a group from the Singapore Ministry of Social and Family Development. The team was looking for a system it could adopt that would address trauma in children they were serving.

As the team members observed presentations throughout the conference, one of the presentations that caught their eyes was the one presented by Kelly and Dr. Brown. Before the delegation returned to Singapore, they requested to visit programs in some different states based on trauma presentations they liked. Subsequently, they came to visit our programs in Kansas. They observed how we had integrated our trauma services into all of our programming. Others had demonstrated their research projects, but the ministry team was impressed with how KVC had fully integrated our research into actual practice in an applied setting with literally thousands of foster children. In addition, they were extremely impressed with our safe reduction of residential usage. Theirs is a system based on orphanages where children grow up in residential care. They were intent upon changing this culture.

This group returned to Singapore, and subsequently other groups and individuals were sent to observe not only our case managers but our inpatient staff. During their first visit, I shared how our organization had started, as well as our vision for carrying out our mission. They were interested and began to tell me and our team how they did not have a foster care or adoption program. They explained how their providers kept the children pretty much until adulthood.

In the process, some Singapore providers, graduate interns, and others from the ministry actually came to observe how we delivered services. Change is hard, but it was apparent that leadership in the ministry wanted to initiate change in their approach to children without families. My eventual personal meetings with the minister proved to be very educational for me. I found him and certainly others in the ministry to be very respectful of all their population.

Currently, Singapore is the second densest sovereign state in the world with a population approaching six million people. Their demographics demonstrate that they are a multiracial and multicultural country composed of Chinese (74.1 percent), Malay (13.3 percent), Indian (9.1 percent), and some Eurasian residents.

The ministry staff's continued interest in the KVC service delivery system eventually resulted in an invitation for certain KVC leadership to travel to Singapore to present at the ministry's annual conference. I was honored to be asked to provide the keynote address to this conference, held in October of 2014; I subsequently delivered a 90-minute presentation. Unlike other conferences I have attended or where I was asked to speak, I found this one to be very formal and precise. From a location in the back of the room, I was given different lights signifying how long I had presented. The lights culminated in a final 10-minute, five-minute, and one-minute light. Amazingly, I was able to stop at the designated time. Some people who know me found that a bit hard to believe, but nonetheless it was true. Others who attended with me were Anne Roberts, Kelly McCauley, and Dr. Adam Brown, and they also can attest to my timely presentation. I may have been much timelier than Kelly and Dr. Brown during their presentations.

Anne Roberts accompanied me, knowing the KVC program and cultural development extremely well, and served with me on other panels that week with members of the ministry and with provider meetings. I was extremely honored to attend a reception the minister held for us, as well as to attend a private meeting with him. He and his staff were very sensitive regarding cultural and religious differences among Singaporean people. As a result, we were invited to visit some of the provider facilities. Because the children essentially grew up in these facilities, they were basically orphanages, although they were not called that. During our stay, we had the opportunity to visit both Christian and Muslim facilities. In both talking with and observing the children in these facilities, the children appeared both physically healthy and friendly. At the Muslim facility, the children were very cute and polite, appearing in matching silk tops and bottoms. I was called "Big Boss" by the children, a title Anne had suggested to them while visiting their facility. I was also asked several times if I knew President Obama. Their questions were worded like, "Hey, Big Boss, you know Obama?" These visits made me even more determined to help Singapore create a shift from their current model to a family-based model, knowing that children grow best in families.

About halfway through the week, I began being questioned about durian fruit. Almost everyone I had already met, plus many I was still meeting for the first time, began asking me if I had tried durian fruit. That question was immediately followed by the comment, "You'll either love it or hate it. There is no in between." Of course, I had never tried it, so our host, who had obviously been assigned to drive us from one event to the next, promised to provide some of the fruit for us to try. I should add that every time I was asked if I had tried the fruit, I asked that person what category they fell into: love it or hate it. The answer was pretty much universal. They loved it. But equally universal, they indicated the smell was horrific, and in fact the fruit had been banned on all means of public transit in Singapore due to its foul odor. My best description of the smell was that of turpentine and onions garnished with dirty gym socks.

As promised, following a group dinner the last night we were there, our host took Anne, Kelly, Adam, and me to try the fruit. We drove to what he described as an undesirable part of the city. As a descriptor of the area, our host said that we might see homeless people and ladies of ill repute. Actually, we saw neither, but we did notice the area was far less maintained than other neighborhoods. We stopped at what looked like a bleacher-style open market where you could climb up several levels while searching for a ripe durian. The man helping us pulled out a large knife and hacked into about three durian fruits before picking the best one for us. Then, each of us was given a pair of clear plastic gloves to wear while we tried the fruit so that our hands would not reek of the smell. The texture was smooth and a bit creamy, something distantly similar to an overripe cantaloupe. My description probably does not do it justice, but they were right about the smell. And, oh by the way, I neither loved it nor hated it, and my colleagues felt similarly.

When we initially went to Singapore, we were finalizing a four-year contract with them. That contract has now been extended. James Roberson has had the honor of providing extensive consultation to some of their provider facilities. I know he, like all of us, has felt both the honor and responsibility to deliver the best training possible. The world shrinks when people of separate countries are able to come together and learn from one another. As Ralph Waldo Emerson said, "The invariable mark of wisdom is to see the miraculous in the common."

---

## "The invariable mark of wisdom is to see the miraculous in the common."

— Ralph Waldo Emerson —

---

It was a true honor and tremendous privilege to be invited to Singapore and to work together with many talented staff of the ministry.

# 24

## Innovations Institute

Over the years, KVC has been asked to provide professional training on many topics in numerous states and in other countries. Singapore is the prime example of another country. But first, as we progressed by spreading our training mission into different states, certain trainings were wanted or needed more than others as each state evolved in a little faster or slower progression. KVC employees from throughout the country were being asked more and more to train state employees and staff members from various provider organizations. Some of our staff members had been asked to conduct workshops at state and national conferences, and in some cases, they were asked to give keynote presentations.

In order to advance our already-occurring "Institute Without Walls" concept, pulling expertise from throughout the KVC system, we felt we needed a forum through which we could continually provide research and collaboration, resulting in cutting-edge care. It would also be a vehicle through which we could track not only the number of trainings being conducted around the country by staff members but track outcomes from research projects in which we were involved. KVC has successfully been able to differentiate our organization from other quality organizations by being involved in numerous research projects in an applied setting. Not only do we provide services, but we do so with the latest research-based strategies. Thus, we felt we needed to create our Innovations Institute.

The emergence of the Institute was long past due in that we have been providing consultation for years.

By January of 2016, when I retired, we had been providing trainings for 15 to 20 years. Following our successful outcomes under system reform and, in particular, our safe reduction of residential care to single digits, other states began not only to take notice but to ask for consultation. We were most often approached to provide information regarding these topics. I found it very interesting that following many of these consultations what was asked for most often was additional information regarding our culture in driving reforms. In fact, they would often ask for a list of our isms.

The process of privatization was, and still is to some level, what a number of different states want to learn about. From the earliest stage of privatizing the Kansas child welfare services, state administrators from around the country wanted to learn more about this phenomenon. So initially, the commissioner and the three contractors began presenting this new concept. Later on, however, this learning component became just one of a number of other training components that KVC offered. KVC began offering one research-based service area after another. Early in our history, we focused on parent management trainings and opted for the Parent Management Training Oregon (PMTO) model. Later, we sought out other researchers or purveyors. This was not an easy task, but realizing just how persistent we were, some researchers began bonding with us and assisting us in applying their research within our practice model. Glenn Saxe, MD, was a perfect example of this extrapolation. Around 2008, we first began being trained in Trauma Systems Therapy (TST) and then began deploying this to our therapists across the country. Later, several of our staff members began to adapt Dr. Saxe's approach, with his acceptance and guidance, to develop training models for case managers, foster parents, and adoptive parents. Much of our work in other states and in countries like Singapore is in the application of Dr. Saxe's approach and in our adaptations from his original model.

In the same manner, we approached other researchers. Several years ago, we approached Sue Lohrbach after learning of research she had been conducting in Minnesota. Sue was seeing a very low percentage of children reenter foster care after they had returned home in the area of Minnesota where her model was being utilized. Several of our staff members began reviewing this research and found that this successful approach would fit nicely into our model. Sue trained our staff in using a group decision-making framework for constant review of children's cases with consistent monitoring of risk. As a result, after subscribing to this model for a number of years, we persuaded Sue to join the KVC team not only as a researcher and trainer but to head our new Innovations Institute. Today, Sue and our team of KVC staff members from across the country are continually seeking to raise the bar for service delivery not only across our nation but internationally. The Institute is also researching the latest technology applications as it applies to our behavioral healthcare and child welfare training and consultations. Again, what separates KVC from other quality organizations is the constant research into new and effective approaches that continually move our mission forward and, in doing so, continually raise the training bar in our fields.

I would be remiss if I did not acknowledge the Annie E. Casey Foundation (AECF) for its support of numerous KVC training initiatives. Just one example is their funding for the expansion of our trauma adaptation training to foster parents in other states. Another is the inclusion of KVC in AECF's Provider Exchange, a group of high-achieving private organizations enlisted to share expertise with providers across the nation. I am very appreciative of AECF as well as the support received through state grants, federal SAMHSA grants, and from entities such as the Robert Wood Johnson Foundation, the Greater

Kansas City Healthcare Foundation, and the REACH Foundation. One of our latest research grants was funded by the Robert Wood Johnson Foundation regarding brain science, studying the impact of trauma on children's developing brains.

So what began as a handful of training components for KVC professionals rapidly grew into a variety of child welfare and behavioral healthcare consultations and trainings for external groups. KVC continues to spread its lessons learned in areas such as the KVC model, the impact of trauma, brain science initiatives, and more to serve not only foster care but children, families, and communities at large.

# 25

## Operating in a Political Arena

In any state in which we work, it is the job of the KVC employee to focus on our work with families and not on politics. KVC has enjoyed a long line of continuity in leadership, as shown with our executive and management teams representing long tenures in the fields and specifically with KVC. Political officials and state leadership are often cyclical. We've always been respectful of those in state leadership and in elected state legislative positions and have always listened closely to what they want achieved and tried to be their best partner and their best soldiers. All the while we remember that we are always responsible for providing quality services or care in whatever role KVC plays in a system. Toward this end, we also respectfully introduce alternative ideas and approaches supported by research in an effort to continually raise the bar. Our primary obligation is improving the lives of our clientele and proving it through measurable outcomes. We always keep our eyes on these goals.

It is our job to work with all elected office holders and appointed state officials. We've always felt that our best defense is a good offense. The KVC focus is to do good work, providing the best quality work in all areas we have been contracted to complete. This is exactly what our staff does, regardless of the political environment.

The field of child welfare involves very emotional and complicated family issues. The process that the court and state investigators go through, sometimes resulting in a child being removed from his or her home, is commonly a contentious one. Few parents want their children to be removed from their homes by a court system and placed with a foster family or even with a relative. While families often find it difficult to complain to a judge about a child being removed, it may be easier to call a legislator. There is always a different story, especially when children have been removed from their homes due to abuse or neglect. Families with children removed from their homes sometimes seek out a legislator to use for venting their discontent and of course want their legislator to intervene and help them get their children back. This is very understandable. Most parents will do whatever they can to get their children back. Some legislators take the concerns at face value and want to immediately hold hearings without first reviewing the actual facts of a case. Because state workers, court workers, and state contractor's staff follow laws pertaining to confidentiality that do not allow them to share information about a child or family without parental permission, legislators do not always hear both sides. Legislators need only to get written permission from the legal guardian in order to peruse the entire file. Sometimes family members do not want to have their actual files read, which may provide strong justification for why a judge ruled to have their children removed.

Some legislators are less interested in federal audits and measurable outcomes of the state's overall program and less interested in the very high percentage of cases that tend to resolve well. Some legislators, based on one or two anecdotal stories, want to dismantle decades of progress, possibly to draw personal or political attention and self-promotion. Gratefully, most legislators in states where KVC provides services are interested in following up appropriately on complaints and try to stay abreast of system issues. State and court employees, as well as private contractor staff, appreciate this approach; legislators are always encouraged to listen to constituents with complaints but equally to solicit consent from those who contact them to allow for open files and a full dialogue. Then, with the complete picture, appropriate actions can be taken or not taken. Families need advocates, and legislators can be great advocates. Again, any review of a case should be handled individually so that learning can come to all affiliated with it. It's appreciated as well that most legislators understand the calls they receive often represent a very small percentage of the work and don't judge the entire system based on those few.

# 26

## Lessons Learned

If you've read this far, you know I and the rest of the KVC staff have learned a lot of lessons as our organization has grown and changed. Here are some of the most important of those lessons.

**There will always be change.** However, change should be for continual improvement and not just for change's sake. No matter how progressive we are or how careful we are in our practices, there is always room for improvement. If you're not growing, you're dying. We should all continue to grow in areas such as services, education, experience, and development.

**Never be reluctant to tackle the status quo.** Over time, some practices become enshrined. You must be willing to challenge the existing practices and make the changes you deem necessary, knowing that change is hard. Just one example is system reform shedding light on status quo services such as foster parents not being able to adopt and, therefore, accepting long-term foster care as a permanency plan. It was not hard to see why so few children were adopted and why the failure rate for adopted children was so high in the foster care system in a prior era.

**Base what you do on values.** As Samuel Clemens said, "You're never wrong to do what's right." Believe in what you and your team are doing, and then act accordingly, even if your decision is not a popular one. Remember, time is a good healer. I don't recall any interval in our organizational growth that wasn't preceded by individuals in authority advising us against what we had on the drawing board. For me, that resistance became a badge of courage. When my team and I felt we understood what was needed and believed it was right, we were determined to forge ahead.

---

## "You're never wrong to do what's right."

— Samuel Clemens —

---

**Hire to your values.** Just having a certain graduate degree and training does not guarantee a good employee. It is also extremely important to hire the right individuals based on their values. State laws and accrediting bodies will identify qualifications, but those do not tell you much about the applicant other than their ability to finish a degree. Hiring the wrong person just so you can fill a vacancy — even when you are short staffed and under considerable pressure — is never the right thing.

**There is no bad experience.** Every experience, even one that seems bad at the time, is an opportunity for growth. It is up to each individual on how to interpret his experiences. Crisis represents an opportunity for change; what appears to be negative at the time may very well turn out to be a positive experience.

**Organizations must be able to differentiate themselves.** It is crucial to be able to identify what sets your organization apart from the hundreds or thousands of others providing similar services across the country.

**Constantly identify gaps in services.** Once you identify gaps, be willing to find or create solutions. Very often, these gaps are connected to high-risk and more costly services, so other organizations stay away from them.

Learn to work with those with the greatest needs. Most organizations are only capable of working with or willing to work with the least challenging clients. If you are able to create the expertise to effectively serve those facing the greatest challenges, your services will always be needed. This expertise will allow you to serve clients at every level of care.

**Environmental scanning is important.** National and local trends are always changing. You must stay ahead of trends. In our industry, it always pays to watch for trends in hospital systems because mental health/ behavioral healthcare changes will often follow changes at the medical/ surgical level. Be aware of funding evolutions or laws impacting care delivery. Watch both the for-profit and not-for-profit arenas, and identify characteristics or efficiencies that are applicable to your business.

**Partnering with states' leadership is very important.** In so many states we have observed a blaming posture between child welfare and behavioral healthcare providers and state leadership — each continually pointing fingers at the other for whatever is not working. This is an enormous waste of time and energy. It is important to understand the roles and dynamics of the relationship and move forward to be the best and most innovative in the role you play.

**You need the right board of directors.** It is imperative to have the right individuals on the board of directors and to have a manageable number of board members for decision-making. Board members should be selected for specific and diverse skills, talents, or influence. Board members have certain built-in responsibilities, but their ability to offer quality outside advice was of the greatest benefit to me. Believing that having more board members will enhance fundraising is typically a fallacy. I recommend that boards have no more than nine members. In my opinion, seven or nine members is ideal; the odd number will deter votes ending in ties.

**Succession planning should always be occurring at all levels of leadership.** Ultimate organizational success is predicated on always having the right people on the bus and in the right seats. I have known organizations to spiral downward because they weren't prepared in emergency situations. Depending on your position, always inform your board members or supervisory personnel as to whom you would recommend for your replacement so you are constantly poised for advancement opportunities. Preferably, you will always have at least two suitable candidates you are mindfully training for whatever position you currently hold. This is another facet of the ism *If you're not growing, you're dying.* You must have bench depth in order to be positioned for effective growth.

**Hire to your (or your organization's) weaknesses.** It's been my experience that many people often hire clones of themselves. A blending of personalities, knowledge, and leadership styles is helpful. Assess your weaknesses and the weaknesses of your leadership, and then hire to those weaknesses.

**Whenever possible, hire from within.** Staff members who have proven their understanding of the organization's goals and commitment to its values and who have continually improved their skills under many different circumstances are almost always the best choice for advancement. However, there are times when you need to improve on an organizational weakness by hiring a nationally known individual or professional who brings instant expertise or credibility.

**Staff development is never complete.** Continual learning at all levels of employment is crucial. Special attention should be given to mid-level supervisors. Constant training using the latest researched information is a must.

**Most successful people are brave enough to go above and beyond what others are willing to do.** In my experience, less successful people are often not willing to take on the extra work needed to attain success and are usually not willing to take the big risks that are likely involved. They tend to wait until they are told that change must happen instead of helping to shape the change and lead the charge for change.

# 27

## Passing the Baton

Thirty-five years after I came to the organization, KVC has over 1,400 employees, and we are working with about 60,000 lives annually, not including several large training and consultation contracts both nationally and internationally. Many of our staff members have had the opportunity to consult in various states and to present at national conferences. We have numerous exciting projects in the works that have yet to come to fruition.

Our Innovations Institute allows opportunities for KVC experts from across the country to be a contributing part of that Institute. KVC leaders serve on national boards and think tanks and are active in research projects. Opportunities for providing feedback to Administration for Children and Families' leadership in DC, as well as to state and federal senators and representatives, are all forums for change in which KVC is represented.

KVC is truly a blessed organization. We have a mission that is very focused on improving lives and a vision not only to change the face of those in foster care but to work on behalf of all in need of quality behavioral healthcare. Our work in trauma and brain science is to train all teachers, responders, and community members. Ideally, when confronted with a highly dysregulated child or adult, the response would not be thinking, "What's wrong with that person?" but instead thinking,

"What's happened to that person?" Our new ism *What's happened to that person?* demonstrates that KVC's approach is to want to help rather than want to control, and there is a tremendous difference.

---

♥ KVC-ism

## *What's happened to that person?*

---

I had a great group of "C's" who not only helped to oversee and make all of this happen but also helped me to identify the next generation of leadership. It's important that leadership represents capability from diverse viewpoints in order for the best products to emerge. It requires individuals to look at opportunities and challenges from different approaches and life experiences to best ensure quality decisions.

Each of the new executives has had ample opportunities to prove his or her value to KVC. Erin Stucky is extremely competent. She joined KVC just after college in an entry-level position and then was given multiple leadership opportunities and performed each in an exemplary fashion. She carefully thinks through issues and has a great take-charge-and-deliver mentality as she approaches challenges and new opportunities. As a result, Erin was selected to become chief operations officer. In like fashion, Chad Anderson sought not only to maintain our clinical competence but to raise the clinical services bar by looking at our services through a clinician's eyes. He has excelled in his tireless efforts to always collaborate with our state and community partners and to support our staff toward excellence. Through both calm and traumatic times, Chad is able to rise above challenges and support our wonderful staff toward the goals of excellence in clinical and other outcome achievements. Thus, Chad was asked to accept the role of chief clinical officer. Along with her new colleagues, Marilyn Jacobson brought other characteristics to the table. Marilyn provides a wealth of information, drawing from her extensive leadership experience in state government to her legal and financial expertise as well as her early learning in the military. She is blessed with an abundance of common-sense, which she applies effectively. Talents like these were, at least, some of the reasons Marilyn was selected to join KVC and, ultimately, to become its next CFO.

The new "C's," led by Jason Hooper, have an average of at least 20 years' experience in child welfare with KVC or, in Marilyn's case, even more in the field. They have immense talent and are continually exploring new opportunities that will take KVC into the future with great zeal and inspiration. The future seems bright and limitless given their tenacity and willingness to embrace opportunities. In my opinion, KVC is a miracle that has far exceeded expectations and is staffed by miracle workers who strive very hard to ensure that vulnerable children and families have an opportunity to live and grow in a healthy and safe environment. It was my great pleasure to serve as CEO of KVC for 35 years and to help the organization embrace one major change after another. Now it has become my next great privilege to co-chair the KVC Board of Directors as we continue to seek to enrich and enhance the lives of families in the KVC network of services and beyond.

---

## "It is amazing what you can accomplish if you do not care who gets the credit."

— President Harry Truman —

---

I close by issuing a challenge to our leaders at KVC now and 35 years from now. I close with a comment made by President Harry Truman that I have used often with my leadership: "It is amazing what you can accomplish if you do not care who gets the credit." By working together,

I know our future KVC leaders and employees will continue to create and drive amazing accomplishments in our fields.  ♥

# 28

## The KVC Story:
## Favorite Faces, Memorable Moments

The original Wyandotte house

Wayne shows kids the future Prairie Ridge campus

Board Member Joe Fahey at the Camel Race fundraiser

Wayne with Dick Bond and Kansas City, KS, mayor Jack Reardon

Wayne with Dick Bond and U.S. Senator Nancy Kassebaum

Wayne with U.S. Senator Bob Dole and U.S. Representative Jan Meyers

Senator Bob Dole Delivering Christmas Gifts

Wayne with U.S. Representative Joseph Kennedy II and Ann Roberts

Wayne with Dick Bond and Bill Dunn, Sr.

Wayne with Fred Ball and Frank Devocelle

Wayne with Fred Ball and U.S. Senator Pat Roberts

Board of Directors (circa 2003) with U.S. Senator Pat Roberts

Wayne shows Scott Asner the future site of
KVC's corporate offices and the Ball Conference Center

KVC Prairie Ridge Hospital campus

Wayne with Fred Ball and Dick Bond

Wayne with U.S. Senator Jay Rockefeller of West Virginia and Sherry Love

Founding mothers JoAnn Ball and Ellen McCarthy

Scott and Susan Asner, with Anne Roberts

Community volunteers Betty Crooker and Adele Hall

Wayne with Board Members David Ball and Olathe Mayor Mike Copeland

Groundbreaking for Sims Family Center in Olathe, KS

KVC Sims Family Center

Wayne with Board Member KU Basketball Coach Bill Self

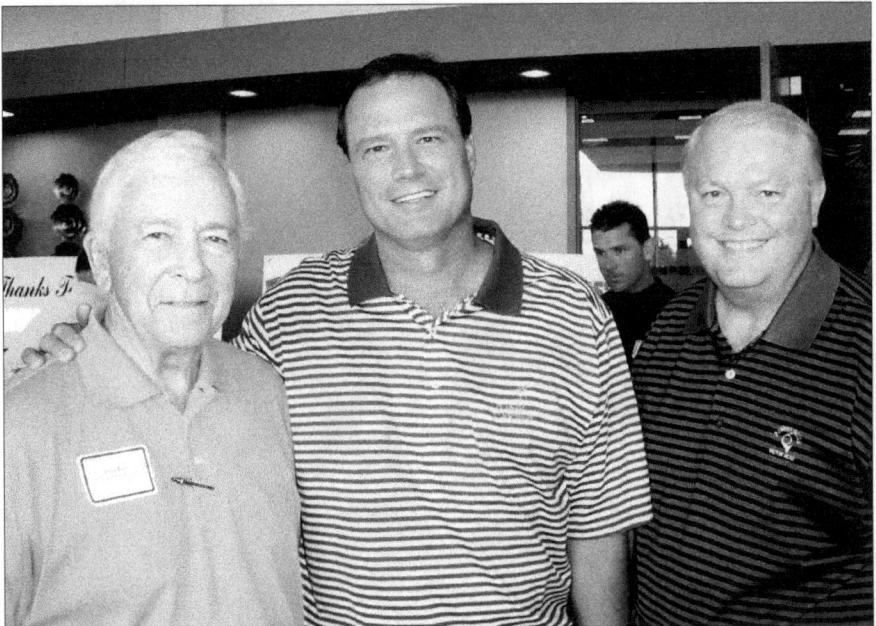

Wayne with Board Members Fred Ball and KU Coach Bill Self

JoAnn and Fred Ball, and their daughters Debbie Simpson and Diane Ball

Wayne with Ellen McCarthy

Wayne with Executive Team Sherry Love, Paul Klayder, and Anne Roberts

Celebration of 40-year history with 40 heroes

Board Members Teresa Markowitz and John Barnes, with Anne Roberts

Wayne with Sherry Love, John Barnes, and Dr. Glenn Saxe

Renny Arensburg and Jason Hooper, with Gala Chair Bonnie Illig and her husband, Cliff

Wayne with David Ball and members of the Dunn Family

Wayne with Jason Hooper and David Ball

Erin Stucky, Anne Roberts, Jason Hooper, Marilyn Jacobson, and Chad Anderson

Wayne with kids at Resource Family Conference

Jim and Esther Sunderland and family members

Management team in Wayne's World ballcaps

Wayne with Sandra Gasca Gonzalez at the White House

Wayne with Board Member Patrick Desbois